NIBBLING ON THE RING

NIBBLING ON THE RING

An Irreverent Culinary Ride

through Wagner's

The Ring of the Nibelung

Morgan Light

Dedicated to the Memory of
Terry McEwen

In the spring of 2011, the San Francisco Opera sent a set of CDs to ticket holders for the summer *Ring* performances. The audio review of *The Ring*'s music and story, originally recorded in 1980, was narrated by Terence A. McEwen, General Director of the SFO from 1982 to 1988. His narration was passionate, personal, and informative, as well as a lot of fun. It was a comment he made about the many potions in Wagner's music dramas that gave me the idea for this book. Thank you, Terry.

CONTENTS

PREFACE

I love opera. It engages all my senses, sends them soaring, and, despite the often simplistic story lines, renews my confidence in humanity. Witnessing opera, I can stop wishing for Batman, Wonder Woman, and Xena Warrior Princess because up there on the stage are *real* super-heroes. Opera singers are able to do something that is super-human: fill a huge space with beautiful sound. Wagnerian singers are the most powerful of these super-heroes, the ones with the biggest voices.

Wagner himself isn't exactly a hero of mine, but writing orchestral music is such an unusual skill that there are even fewer outstanding composers than singers. And Wagner is one of the best. His music has given me a tremendous amount of pleasure and enriched my life. I love sharing my enjoyment. May 22, 2014 marks 201 years since Wagner's birth. This little book is my attempt to share with you and a token celebration of Wagner's bicentennial.

Planning to go to my first live *Ring Cycle*, the sheer length was daunting for me. I wasn't sure I'd be able to stick it out without napping. What a surprise to me that I was on the edge of my seat for the entire time! A month later, I was ready to find tickets for my next live *Ring*. If you get the chance to attend a production of *The Ring Cycle*, grab it!

I promise that if you give yourself the opportunity, you *will* feel the power and beauty of Wagner's *Ring*. No matter what else you may have heard about Wagner the ego-maniac, his politics, or his behavior, you should give the operas some attention. Don't deny yourself the experience of this music because its composer was nuts. You may have heard that the illogical story of *The Ring* is impossible to understand. That may be so—it *is* problematic in places—but *The Ring of the Nibelung* is a phenomenal work and the beauty and power of the music will amply repay you for whatever time you invest.

Even though the plot is complicated and loses continuity in places, familiarity with the story can help your thorough enjoyment of the music. That's where this book comes in. I am adding to that glut of information, but with a flavorful twist. Here you will not find any discussion about Wagner's personality, his rambling writings, or his political legacy. Discussion of the *leitmotifs* is included, but this is not musical analysis; in fact many of the musical samples are simplified. Traditional Wagnerites may take offense if they feel everything Wagnerian 𝔐𝔲𝔰𝔱 𝔅𝔢 𝔖𝔢𝔯𝔦𝔬𝔲𝔰. This book definitely is not serious, it is the story of *The Ring* made fun. The two things that make life worth living, music and food, are my main concerns. The guide is meant to be a vehicle for you to enjoy a ride through *The Ring Cycle* with stops along the way when the inspiration for a recipe strikes.

What could be better than amazing music accompanied by tasty food? Anyway, birthday cake is so trite.

Hoyotoho!
May, 2014

INTRODUCTION
For Ring Rookies

The Ring of the Nibelung, also known as *The Ring* or *The Ring Cycle*, is a series of four operas by Richard Wagner: *The Rhinegold, The Valkyrie, Siegfried,* and *Twilight of the Gods.** Wagner wrote the libretto and the music and then had a special theatre constructed where the dramas could be performed as he wished. The text was begun in 1848 and Wagner worked on it fairly regularly until 1857. By that time he had finished the entire libretto and composed the music of *The Rhinegold, The Valkyrie,* and the first two acts of *Siegfried.* Twelve years later, in 1869, he resumed work on the Cycle and the music was completed in 1872. After several years of fund raising, his theatre in Bavaria near Munich, the Bayreuth Festspielhaus, was built and *The Ring* was performed as a whole for the first time in August of 1876—28 years after he began formulating his idea.

Wagner's concept of opera was different from earlier operatic works. His idea was to create something that meshed all the arts into one piece, what he called a *Gesamtkunzwerk*, or "complete artistic work," loosely modeled on ancient Greek theatre. He employed stories and characters from ancient mythology to provide a cultural background that most Northern Europeans could relate to. Writing *The Ring*, he used *Das Niebelungenlied* as inspiration. The German text dates from the 11th century. However, its origins are found in earlier Viking sources and Icelandic and Norse *eddas*, or sagas. He used the stories as a starting point and changed things freely to make the characters and events fit his own ends. To sustain dramatic tension, Wagner dispensed with the old operatic model of arias and recitative in favor of continuous music from the beginning to the end of each act. The orchestra was intended to be a sort of additional character, portraying the psychological subconscious or emotions related to what is going on in the story.

The operas, or "Music Dramas" as Wagner referred to his works, are among the largest-scale musical works in the Western repertoire. For *The Ring*, the orchestras are gigantic, about 100 pieces, and the casts are very large, ranging from 8 to 14 named characters with individual parts. Most productions present the four operas over several days. The length of each drama

---

* The original German titles are *Der Ring des Nibelungen: Das Rheingold, Die Walküre, Siegfried,* and *Götterdämmerung.*

stretches the limits of human attention and sitting power: from two and one-half hours for *The Rhinegold* (no intermission that night) to the almost six-hour duration of *Twilight of the Gods* including its two intermissions.

From the performers' standpoint, the work is among the most demanding of all operas. For example, the singer who portrays Siegfried must be a *heldentenor* (heroic tenor), a powerful singer with a range of more than two octaves and immense stamina. In *Siegfried* he sings, with a few pauses, for about four and one-half hours, the last 30 minutes of which is a lengthy duet with a soprano who shows up at that point fresh as a daisy. All singers in the cast must have extremely powerful voices just to be heard above the large orchestra. The orchestra members must be attentive to their craft for hours at a stretch, performing some of the most difficult passages in orchestral music. Perhaps the most amazing feat is that of the conductor who must sustain his or her concentration and intense passion without pause for the duration of each act.

Wagner intentionally used devices to engage the audience members' psychology. The best known of these devices is the *leitmotif*, the "leading motive," or musical theme. In this book, I will use the word "motif" to refer to these short musical themes. A motif may denote a character, an object, or an event, or it may carry connotations for emotion. Wagner's motifs are not mere elements of typical program music. The motifs evolve through the Cycle, becoming more than simple indicators. They are intended to link elements of the story at a subtle level of consciousness. The *leitmotif* topic is the subject of many books and articles by critics, musicologists, philosophers, and psychologists. The motifs are complicated enough to keep an expert occupied for years. Even for the unsuspecting amateur, they have a mysterious appeal that can fascinate and captivate.

Here is an example of the development of a motif through the cycle, the first section of the Joy in the Gold motif. These are only a few examples of the many forms taken by this little theme.

It begins as the cheerful two-chord passage sung by the Rhine Maidens:

Later in Act Two of *Rhinegold* the orchestra plays a darker version of it while Loge is telling the story of the Ring's fabrication:

The Tarnhelm motif bears an eerie resemblance to the beginning of the Joy in the Gold motif, emphasizing the evil use Alberich has made of the gold.

At the end of *Rhinegold* the Rhine Maidens lament the loss of their gold:

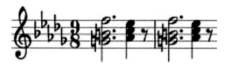

During Hagen's "Watch Song" at the end of Scene Two of Act One *Twilight of the Gods*, the chords take on a deeper dissonance, depicting the obsession that the devious Hagen has for the Ring.

In Act Two of *Twilight*, Hagen bellows out this call, full of his avid hunger for the Ring.

As you can see, these two chords gradually and profoundly develop throughout the four dramas. They are transformed from the buoyant harmony sung by the Rhine Maidens celebrating the beauty and purity of the Rhinegold into the progressively tragic dissonances denoting the suffering caused by the Ring made from that gold.

This book is a far cry from musical analysis, but the motifs are an important part of *The Ring*, so simplified snippets of the score have been transcribed and included as they relate to the story.

While researching the details of *The Ring*, I came across many wonderful portraits of singers from the productions since 1876. These sent me off on an exploration for illustrations and photographs over 70 years old, and therefore out of copyright, to enhance the text and to share with you. Some of these are truly fabulous and add a hint of the appeal and the fascination that these ancient legends have inspired.

I have translated everything except the names of characters into English. Accordingly, the operas are referred to by their English titles, not the original German titles. The lyrics that accompany motifs remain in German because the English doesn't fit into the music and because the excerpts can be more easily recognized from the German words while you are listening to a recording. The German lyrics are translated into English in the book's text.

Speaking of listening to a recording, please do so. Although the operas are not completely understandable solely from the music, the music is what makes the *Ring Cycle* profound. If you don't own a recording, borrow one from a friend or library. If you can't find the whole cycle, at least listen to excerpts that you can locate on Internet sites such as youtube.com or other similar places. It will be worth the effort.

Recordings of the music, either audio or video, make terrific kitchen companions. A recording can help you warble your way through the recipes. It is really great fun and it is my pleasure to share this with you.

GUIDE TO CHARACTERS

Divine and non-human characters

Wotan (voe-tahn) is the chief god. He is also known as Wälse (vel-seh) and Wanderer.

Fricka (rhymes with "trick ah") is the goddess of family and marriage who upholds traditional values. She is Wotan's wife.

Freia (fry-ah) is the goddess of youth and beauty, and the cultivator of the Golden Apples. She is Fricka's sister.

Froh (rhymes with "flow") is the god of joy and sunshine—you know, stuff like puppies and rainbows. He is a brother of Fricka and Freia.

Donner (just like the reindeer) is the god of thunder. He is the brother of Fricka, Freia, and Froh.

Loge (low-guh) is the personification of fire. A demi-god, he does not share the residence—or the fate—of the gods.

The Rhine Maidens are the three daughters of the Rhine River. They guard the Rhinegold, the precious luster, sparkle, and purity of the river.

Erda (air-dah) is the all-knowing Earth goddess. She lives underground and sleeps in order to dream. Her dreams inform her of the future.

The Norns (rhymes with horns) are Erda's three daughters. They take the "threads" of Erda's knowledge of the future and weave it into a "rope" of destiny. The Norns are roughly equivalent to the Greek Fates Clotho, Lachesis, and Atropos, but with the boring names of First Norn, Second Norn, and Third Norn.

Alberich (all-ber-ic) and Mime (mee-muh) are Nibelung (nee-bel-lung) brothers from Nibelheim (nee-bel-hime). The Nibelungs are dwarfish miners who live underground. Alberich sets the tale in motion by stealing the Rhinegold. Although Alberich and Mime are brothers, they have a hostile relationship.

Fasolt (fass-solt) and Fafner (fahf-ner) are the last of the race of the Giants. They are the brothers who built Valhalla, a combination castle and fortress, for Wotan.

The Valkyries (val-keer-ee) are Wotan's daughters who bring fallen heroes back from battlefields and revive them to guard Valhalla. There are nine of them: Brünnhilde (broon-hilda), Waltraute (vahl-trout-eh), and their seven sisters who all have similarly long, Teutonic names. Brünnhilde is Wotan's favorite daughter and the heroine of *The Ring*.

Grane (grah-neh) is Brünnhilde's horse.

Human characters

Wälse (vehl-zeh) was Wotan's name when he lived on the earth as a human and sired the Wälsung twins. Wälse and Wälsung are translated as "wolf." Wagner used the symbol of the wolf to relate Wotan to his earlier incarnation of the Norse god Odin who ran around accompanied by two wolves. Siegmund refers to his intrepid father as "a wolf to fearful foxes."

Siegmund (zeeg-moond) is the heroic son of Wotan and a nameless mortal woman.

Sieglinde (zeeg-lin-deh) is Siegmund's twin sister.

Hunding (hoon-ding) is Sieglinde's legal husband.

Siegfried (zeeg-freed) is the heroic son of Sieglinde and Siegmund, the hero of *Siegfried* and *Twilight of the Gods*.

Hagen (haa-ghen as in Häagen Dazs) is the son of Alberich. He is the antagonist in *Twilight of the Gods*.

Gunther (goon-ter) is the king of the Gibichungs, people who live along the Rhine River. Gunther is the half-brother of Hagen.

Gutrune (goo-troo-neh) is Gunther's sister, noted for being easily manipulated by her brother and half-brother.

Gibich (ghib-bish) was the founder of the Gibichung Empire and the father of Gunther and Gutrune. Evidently he was naive and gullible, traits he passed to his unfortunate children.

Grimhilde (grim-hil-deh) was the mother of Hagen, and later the wife of Gibich and mother of Gunther and Gutrune. She was a power-hungry social climber who accepted a bribe from Alberich to bear a son for him and subsequently used a magic potion to attract and marry Gibich. She bequeathed her magic potion to Hagen who uses it against Siegfried.

Other elements

Valhalla, in a general sense, is the dwelling place of the gods. Specifically, it is their magnificent edifice built by the Giants.

Nothung (no-toong) is the sword that Wotan first creates, and then shatters, in *The Valkyrie*. Siegfried reforges it and then uses it to kill the dragon in *Siegfried*. It symbolizes valor, truth, and honor. The word *Nothung* is always translated into English as the noun "need." It is a variation of the German word *nötig*, which indicates something that is required or needed. Siegmund gives the sword this name when he is in a situation of great peril and need, or *nöt* in German.

Wotan's spear symbolizes Wotan's authority and serves as the portable filing cabinet where he keeps the records of contracts and agreements that sustain his power. The spear was created by Wotan from a branch of the World Ash Tree.

Weltesche (velt-esh-eh), The World Ash Tree, known as *Yggdrasil* in Norse mythology, is the Vikings' primeval Tree of Life whose branches reach to the heavens and whose roots reach to the underworld. It is a protector of the world and, in some Norse myths, the world actually rests on it. Wagner borrowed this symbol, along with several others from Norse mythology, for *The Ring Cycle*. In *Twilight of the Gods* we learn that after Wotan cut a branch from the tree, it lost its leaves, withered, and eventually died. It is cut into logs and used as fuel for the fire at the end of this final opera.

THE RHINEGOLD

It was Wagner's intention to tell the story of a mythic place from its creation to its destruction. This opera, and the whole cycle, starts with this world's creation: a low E-flat.

The Beginning

This goes on for a while and then develops into the Nature Motif that depicts the natural world. Many of the motifs in the cycle develop from this basic motif.

Nature Motif

As the curtain rises the music's tempo increases to emulate the sound of surging water. It is the Rhine River and we are introduced to the Rhine Maidens.

Scene One

The Rhine Maidens, three air-headed sopranos, were left in charge of the Rhine's gold by their father, but who and where the Rhine Father is—and why he left these goofy girls in charge—we are left on our own to wonder. The Rhine Maidens swim around singing until the low woodwinds alert us that something disturbing is about to happen. Alberich the Nibelung, a dwarf from Nibelheim, clambers up from his underground caves to see what he can see. He is attracted to the svelte Rhine Maidens and tries to grab them. The Rhine Maidens are fast and slippery. They tease ugly Alberich unmercifully until a shaft of sunlight reflects off something shiny and a horn from the orchestra, later echoed by a trumpet, tells us we are witnessing the precious Rhinegold.

Gold Fanfare

That is how we know it is time for:

Rhinegold Mashed Potatoes

A few threads of saffron

6 Yukon Gold potatoes

1 yam or sweet potato

½ cup milk

2 tbs. butter

1 tbs. brown sugar (optional)

Salt to taste

White and cayenne pepper to taste

Paprika for color

- Peel the potatoes and cut into big chunks. Bring a large saucepan of water to a boil. The water should cover the potatoes. Sprinkle the saffron into the water to help the potatoes turn a good golden color. (If you don't have saffron, you can use turmeric.) Boil the potatoes until soft, about 25 minutes.
- Drain the potatoes and set aside 10-12 of the chunks. Mash the rest of the potatoes to your preferred consistency.
- Heat the milk and butter on the stove or in the microwave until the butter is melted and the milk is warm, about 30-45 seconds in the microwave. Add the sugar to the milk mixture and stir until dissolved.
- Stir the milk into the mashed potatoes and add the salt and pepper.
- Sculpt a Rhinegold shape from the mashed potatoes, using the reserved chunks as "nugget" accents. Sprinkle with paprika to mimic the gold's sparkle.
- Makes 6 servings, about ½ cup each.

Rhinegold potatoes are best enjoyed while the Rhine Maidens sing "Rhinegold! Rhinegold! La-la-la-la-la," the Joy in the Gold Motif.

Joy in the Gold Motif

Rhein - gold! Rhein - gold! Hei - a - ja - hei - a! Hei - a - ja - hei - a!

Sing along with them but, please, not with a mouth full of mashed potatoes.

Alberich has not heard of the Rhinegold. He asks what it is that gleams and shines. The Rhine Maidens explain, after chiding and belittling him, that it is the Rhinegold—have you been living under a rock? Well, yes, he has. Alberich says in essence, "So what? What good is it?" The Rhine Maidens reply that if someone were able to make a ring from the gold, it would give the maker boundless wealth and power. The catch is described by the Love-Curse Motif:

Renunciation of Love or Love-Curse Motif

Nur wer der Min - ne Macht ent - sagt, nur wer der Lie - be Lust ver - jagt,

. . . "only one who renounces love, who drives away love's desire," would be able to create a ring from the Rhinegold.

Alberich, smarting from the Rhine Maidens' taunts and teasing—and evidently just as love-starved in Nibelheim—decides that since no one loves him anyway, he will repudiate love and steal the gold to make a ring. After all, he is a miner and master metal smith; if anyone can craft a ring from the gold, he should be able to do it.

Musically, there is a lot going on in these few minutes. When Alberich puts his grubby mitts on the gold, we hear the foreboding minor-key Rhinegold Fanfare. He proclaims a curse on love, an altered form of the Love-Curse Motif. Ultimately, the orchestra's undercurrent develops into the definitive Power of the Ring Motif, which will appear many times in many forms throughout the cycle.

Minor Fanfare Variation

Alberich Curses Love

| so | ver - fluch' | ich | die | Lie | - | be! |
| love | hence - forth | be | ac - curs | - | ed! |

Ring Motif

In a nutshell, Alberich curses love, grabs the gold, and runs off. The Rhine Maidens swim around helplessly, wailing and lamenting at the end of Scene One.

The Rhine Maidens in the first Bayreuth production of Wagner's Ring cycle in 1876.
Photographer unknown. Public domain.

Scene Two

Scene Two is our introduction to the CEO of the gods, Wotan. Wotan is a baritone; the singer who portrays him is usually quite tall and imposing. He wears a patch over one eye, carries his spear with him, and struts around as if he is the embodiment of law and honor. His spear holds a record of his contracts and agreements. The source of the spear is not explained by Wagner until the fourth opera, *Twilight of the Gods*, but Wotan created it through an act of violence to the World Ash Tree. In the story of *The Ring*, the World Ash Tree never recovers from the loss of the branch from which Wotan made his spear. So, although he would like everybody to think of him as an honorable leader, we already know that he is not above grabbing what he wants without considering the consequences.

Wotan's wife is Fricka, a goddess whose wisdom he so earnestly wanted to share that he wagered his good eye for her. Fricka is the goddess of home, marriage, and family. She has many divine relatives, some of whom we will meet shortly. Her role in *The Ring* is to serve as the proponent of tradition and conventional values.

Wotan and Fricka are waking up with the dawn. They have been asleep on a rock waiting for the completion of their new home, a sort of combined castle and fortress. Although it is not named until the end of *The Rhinegold*, we know this is Valhalla. Where the gods lived pre-Valhalla is a mystery that is not addressed by Wagner. Did these high, mighty, supposedly wise gods just hang out on a rock? Why don't they at least have a tent and sleeping bags? But without explanation they are just out there alone on a rock, waking up. The orchestral music introduces us to Valhalla.

Valhalla Motif

As they wake up, Wotan and Fricka can see through the parting mist that the castle is finished. The castle has been built by the giants Fasolt and Fafner. The brother giants were contracted to build Valhalla by Wotan and the agreement can be found recorded on Wotan's spear. Fricka reminds Wotan that the price he agreed to pay the giants is—can we be hearing this correctly?—her sister Freia, the goddess of love and youth. What kind of a god pays for a castle with a goddess? But Wotan says he was never serious about giving Freia to the giants. Rather, he has been working on a plan to find something else that the Giants will prefer to Freia.

Just then Freia runs out onto the rock. "Help! Help!" she pleads as she runs away from big, ugly Fasolt. Seemingly oblivious to her plight, Wotan only asks if she has seen Loge, the tricky god of fire. Freia is surely thinking, "Holy mackerel, here I come, running away from these horrible giants, in danger of my life and chastity, and all you can say is *"Where's Loge?"'* Wotan explains that he has sent Loge out into the world to find a substitute payment. Loge promised to find a way to set Freia free.

Loud, plodding music from the percussion, basses, and low brass alert us that the giants are about to make their appearance.

Giants' Motif

Fasolt sings, "While you gods and goddesses were lounging around getting your beauty sleep, Fafner and I were working very hard on this castle for you. Now we have finished and we want to be paid."

Wotan, as if he didn't know any better, asks them to name their wage. Fasolt is surprised that Wotan seems to have forgotten and reminds him of their discussion about Freia going with the giants in exchange for their labor.

Fafner speaks up. "What did I tell you? See how deceptive these gods are?"

Fasolt is in love with Freia and is looking forward to having her as his wife. He says that although he may be stupid and dimwitted compared to the gods, he knows that Wotan cannot act against the contracts inscribed upon his spear.

Fafner chides his brother for being sentimental. He does not feel the same need for female companionship. His motive for taking Freia away from the other gods is to injure them. To the tune of the Golden Apples Motif, Fafner explains the value of Freia's apples. "Golden apples grow in her garden." Only she knows how to care for the apples.

Golden Apples Motif

Gold' - ne Aep - fel   wach - sen in ih - rem Gar - ten

It is the apples that allow the gods to keep their eternal youth and only Freia can grow them. Without Freia, there will be no apples; without the apples, the gods will grow old and weak and eventually become powerless.

Wotan and the giants argue together for a few lines until the giants, impatient, demand that Freia go with them.

Freia is freaking out and calls for her brothers Froh and Donner to help protect her from the giants. They appear to this triumphant passage:

Mighty Mouse [1]

Oh, sorry, not that one. This one:

The Entrance of Froh and Donner

But Froh and Donner cannot save the day because the agreement between Wotan and the Giant Brothers is inscribed on Wotan's spear. As keeper of the law, Wotan insists that the other gods leave the giants alone and let him handle the negotiations. Meanwhile, he is getting very impatient for Loge to come and help him weasel out of his predicament. The orchestra tells us Loge is on his way by the fast and furious passages played by the strings followed by the flickering notes of the piccolo. Finally, he shows up.

Loge takes his time explaining how difficult his task was. He reports that he has finally found one thing that a man (or a giant) might agree to take in place of a woman's "bliss and worth." He tells the story of Alberich and the stolen Rhinegold. In his anecdote, he includes a bit about the Rhine Maidens who yammer night and day for their lost treasure and how they continually entreat Wotan to help them get it back. Loge describes what has occurred between the end of Scene One and the beginning of Scene Two: Alberich has managed to amass an enormous hoard of gold and treasure after making the Ring from the Rhinegold and enslaving the Nibelungs.

Loge thinks the best way to get the gold from Alberich is by theft. Good idea; they should just use thievery to get the gold from the thief who stole it from the Rhine Maidens. When he mentions the Rhine Maidens again, he points out that they have begged Loge to appeal to Wotan on their behalf.

Fasolt and Fafner are intrigued by the story of the gold. In addition to the power that it holds, they like the idea of obtaining it because they resent and hate Alberich. It is alarming to them that the sneaky little Nibelung is gaining so much power; they have no doubt that Alberich will do what he can to make the giants' lives miserable. So they tell Wotan that if he can get the hoard of gold for them, they will let Freia go. But until then, they will hold Freia hostage. Fasolt, Fafner, and Freia leave to sounds of lamenting (Freia), threats (Froh), and curses (Donner).

Immediately the gods on the rock sink into a funk. They lose their vitality and suddenly feel old. Loge explains (Wagner probably does this for our benefit—you would think the gods already know this) that without Freia, they will not get their daily youth-fruit. Freia, guardian of the orchard where the Golden Apples grow, must be around for the daily harvest of apples and for the gods to maintain their immortality. Without Freia and her fruit, the gods will turn old and gray, gloomy and morose, and eventually they will perish.

After such a dire prediction, we had better stop for a bite of apple ourselves.

The Goddess Freia under a tree of her Golden Apples. Arthur Rackham (1867-1939). Public domain.

Freia's Golden Apple Risotto

5 cups water

2 tbs. "Better than Bouillon" organic mushroom base (other bouillon or stock can be used, but this is really yummy)

4 tbs. butter

2 tbs. minced onion

1 cup Arborio rice

2-3 cups peeled and diced apples (Freia is partial to Honeycrisp, but any will work. Use 3 to 4 apples if they are large like Golden Delicious, 4 to 6 of a smaller variety like Pink Lady.)

4 tbs. dry white wine

2 tbs. (plus a little more for sprinkling on top) grated Parmesan or Romano cheese

Salt and nutmeg to taste

- Heat the water to boiling and add the bouillon, then reduce the heat to simmer and cover.
- In another large pan, sauté the onion in some of the butter for a few minutes, until the onion is translucent. Add the rice and half the diced apples. Sauté a few minutes more, then add the wine and stir until the liquid has evaporated.
- Add ½ to 1 cup of the hot bouillon to the rice mixture. There should be enough just to cover the rice. The heat should be enough to hold the mixture at a simmer.
- Stirring constantly, cook the rice until the broth is absorbed, 3 to 5 minutes.
- Add bouillon by the ½ cup, stirring and letting the rice absorb the liquid after each addition. Stir in the rest of the apples just before you add the last of the bouillon. The rice should be *al dente*, creamy and firm. If there is still a little crunch, add broth or water until it is perfect. Don't add too much; it shouldn't be mushy.

- Remove the risotto from the heat and stir in the rest of the butter and 2 tbs. Romano cheese. Sprinkle salt to taste. Dish onto plates or serving platter, and sprinkle with some more cheese and a little nutmeg.
- Serve immediately.

Although we are refreshed from our taste of golden apples, the gods are still languishing. Even so, Wotan snaps out of his despondency and urges Loge on to Nibelheim so they can steal Alberich's hoard of gold and get Freia back.

Scene Three

We are not told how much time has elapsed between Alberich stealing the gold and Wotan and Loge's descent to Nibelheim. But during this interval, Alberich the master metal smith has been able to craft a magical Ring from the Rhinegold. As the Rhine Maidens foretold, the Ring has given him immense power. With his newfound power, he has enslaved the Nibelungs who now cower before him and do his bidding. They mine for gold and jewels and Alberich has amassed an enormous hoard of precious treasure.

I have not experienced vast power, nor have I engaged with people who hurry to fulfill my every wish. The only time that even comes close is after people taste my almond cheesecake. Watch your guests after you offer it and see if they groan with pleasure from their first taste and offer to reward you handsomely if you will bake one for their next party. If there is a dessert that can grant power, this may be it.

To resemble Alberich's Ring for this photograph, I cut a circle out of the center of the cake and decorated it with gold food coloring

Limitless Power Over the World Cheesecake

3 8-ounce bricks of cream cheese (Use regular cream cheese. Low-fat cream cheese will not yield a good texture.)

1 cup sugar

3 large eggs

½ tsp. vanilla extract

1 tsp. pure almond extract

Ground almonds, almond meal, or whole almonds

Roll of marzipan or almond paste

- Preheat oven to 300°. Do not use convection bake.
- Prepare a 10'' springform pan:
  - Press the ground almonds into the bottom for the crust. If you are starting with whole nuts, you can grind them in a coffee grinder ¼ to ⅓ cup at a time. (I make this and other nut recipes often, so I have two coffee grinders: one for coffee beans and one for nuts. That way I don't get coffee-flavored ground nuts.) Prepared ground almond flour, sometimes called almond meal, is available from some grocery stores.
  - Use a cheese slicer to shave off about ten or twelve thin slices of the marzipan and lay them over the nuts.
- Unwrap the cream cheese and put in the mixer bowl. With a heavy-duty mixer or by hand, beat the cream cheese until soft and smooth.
- Add the sugar and continue mixing.
- Add the eggs one at a time, stopping the mixer and scraping the bowl after each egg.
- Add the vanilla and almond extracts and mix well again.
- Carefully spread the batter over the almond and marzipan crust.
- Bake at 300° for about an hour, until the top of the cake is a light golden brown.

- Make the topping:
  1 cup sour cream (here you can use a low-fat variety if you want)
  ⅔ cup powdered sugar
  1 tbs. vanilla extract (or mixture of vanilla and almond extracts)
  Pinch of salt
    - Mix these four ingredients together, beating until smooth.
- When the cake is cool, spread the topping on it and decorate with almonds.

Mmm, high-fat heaven. Now back to our story.

We first witness the power of Alberich's Ring at the beginning of Scene Three, where Alberich is beating his brother Mime and insisting that he produce the helmet that Alberich had ordered. This chainmail helmet is known as the Tarnhelm (camouflage helmet). Mime has completed its fabrication. Alberich snatches it, puts it on his head and becomes invisible.

Tarnhelm Motif

This makes things even worse for Mime because now he can't see where Alberich's blows will come from next. Alberich is delighted with his new toy and wanders off to try it out on other Nibelung victims.

To be precise, those goofy Rhine Maidens told Alberich that the Ring would convey not just enormous wealth and power, but *unlimited* wealth and power. It is difficult to overlook the fact that unlimited power would probably have prevented the events that follow. However, we must ignore it and proceed.

Wotan and Loge descend to Nibelheim and the first person they encounter is Mime. They offer him sympathy—the kind of sympathy shown with crocodile tears—until Alberich shows up driving a crowd of Nibelungs before him admonishing them to "Hurry! Pile up the gold! Don't be lazy! Get back to work!" Screaming in fear, they scatter back to their mine shafts. Mime slips away with them. Alberich notices his visitors and asks what's up.

"We have heard some wild gossip about a treasure down here in Nibelheim and wanted to see for ourselves." Small talk ensues. They discuss the Ring, the enslavement of the Nibelungs, the hoard of gold, and touch on the subject of world domination—you know, the standard subjects of conversation when dwarves and gods get together. Alberich's promise of taking over the world does not threaten Wotan, who is confident of his power over the silly little dwarf. Familiar with Wotan's superior power, Loge does not take Alberich seriously, but he acts as if he does.

When Alberich tells them that the Tarnhelm allows him to assume any shape he wishes, Loge says he doesn't believe it. Alberich proves the power of the Tarnhelm by turning into a serpent before their eyes.

Rhinegold audiences eagerly anticipate the snake—the smaller the production budget, the funnier the snake. Here is my version:

Tarnhelm Chiles Rellenos

1 package crescent rolls refrigerated dough
1 27-ounce can of mild whole green chiles, or fresh poblanos, roasted and peeled
1½ to 2 cups Jack and Cheddar cheese, sliced or shredded
Olives, pimentos, and capers for decorating

- Preheat the oven to 350°.
- With a rolling pin, roll the dough out until it is very thin.
- Cut the dough into rectangles or squares to fit around the chiles.
- Make one slice lengthwise down the whole chile pepper from the pointed tip almost up to the stem. Scrape out stringy stuff and seeds, then fill with a mix of cheeses and fold it back into its original shape.
- Place the pepper on a square of dough and roll the dough around the pepper, folding and smoothing the edges to make them even. Form into a snakey shape.
- Place a small piece of pimento where the tongue should be and seal the dough around one end. Use capers or olives to make eyes.
- Bake at 350° for 25-30 minutes until golden brown.

Rellenos are traditionally served with green or red chile sauce and sour cream.

The orchestra accompanies the appearance of the snake with powerfully scary music. Loge pretends to be terrified of the serpent while Wotan stands off to one side laughing. As the music calms down again, Alberich regains his normal shape, removes the Tarnhelm and says, "So! Now do you believe me?"

Loge exclaims with a fearful demeanor: he was so frightened! He tells Alberich it is amazing, almost unbelievable that the dwarf grew so rapidly into a giant serpent. Then he asks but what if Alberich found himself in a dangerous situation where he needed to run away quickly? Could he change into something small in order to hide from danger?

"Nothing could be easier!" answers Alberich, "How small?" "Oh, say, toad size?" suggests Loge.

Alberich falls for the trick and turns into a toad. Wotan puts his foot on the toad, Loge grabs the Tarnhelm, Alberich reappears struggling under Wotan's foot, and in a flash Loge ties him up. Loge and Wotan drag Alberich out of Nibelheim.

Nibelheim Josef Hoffmann (1831-1904). Public domain.

Scene Four

Back on the rock, Wotan lets Alberich know who is boss. He insists that Alberich pay a ransom for his freedom. Alberich uses the Ring's magic to summon the Nibelungs. They pile the gold up in a heap, scream in terror, and disappear back to Nibelheim. Alberich surrenders the gold to Wotan and prepares to go home, first demanding that Loge return his Tarnhelm.

"Nope," says Loge, "Tarnhelm is part of the ransom," and he throws it on the pile.

Ouch! Alberich hates to part with the gold, but the Nibelungs are still his slaves, so he can make them produce more treasure. He resents and protests the loss of that groovy Tarnhelm, but figures he can trick Mime into making another one. Now he is ready to go home.

"Shall I let him go?" Loge asks Wotan.

Wotan says that the Ring on Alberich's finger also belongs to the ransom; he won't let him go until he relinquishes the Ring. Alberich can't believe it, he'd rather they take his life than the Ring. But Wotan won't take no for an answer and forcibly seizes the Ring from Alberich's finger. After savoring his victory for a moment, Wotan tells Loge to untie Alberich and send him away.

However, Alberich has a little something to say before he leaves:

"Am I free? Really free? Then let this be my freedom's greeting to you! I leave this curse here with the Ring. Here is my freedom's word: Whoever has the Ring will be destroyed by the fear of losing it. Envy will consume anyone who wants the Ring."

Here is Alberich's Curse Motif:

Curse Motif

The actual curse is much longer and full of nasty-sounding German guttural sounds. It is sung in Alberich's powerful baritone, loud and creepy. Scary stuff.

Almost everybody is unnerved by this curse. Wotan, however, says, "Pfft, let him fume."

Presently, Fafner and Fasolt return with Freia. The gold is very attractive to Fafner, but Fasolt is still hesitant to accept it in exchange for the goddess whom he loves. He says that the gold must be piled up in front of Freia so that he cannot see her anymore.

"More! More! Fill the little gaps!" he and Fafner shout. Froh, Donner, and Loge shape a pile in front of Freia until all the gold is used up. Fafner says they can still see her hair but if the Tarnhelm is added to the pile, it will hide her hair. So the Tarnhelm is added to the hoard.

Fasolt laments, "Must I lose her?" and peeks through the treasure pile. "While I can still see her starry eye, I will not let her go." Fasolt can still see that sweet eye, but there is no more gold.

"What about that Ring?" asks Fafner.

Loge explains that the Ring does not belong to Wotan, it is the Rhine Maidens' gold and Wotan will return it to them. But Wotan, hearing this, explodes, "What, are you nuts? No way am I giving this Ring back to the Rhine Maidens!"

"Well, OK then, we are back to square one," says Fafner. "We will take Freia home with us as payment." Fricka, Freia, Froh, and Donner let Wotan know this is completely unacceptable and he must give the Ring to the giants.

And—despite knowing about the apples, the curse on the Ring, the pining Rhine Maidens—what does Wotan do? He refuses.

Furious loud music stops suddenly, and mysterious stage lighting and music herald the arrival of Erda, the earth mother. The mysterious music is low and slow, Erda's Motif:

Erda's Motif

Erda rises waist high from a rocky fissure. Is she only about half the height of a regular person? Does she have legs? What does she do underground all the time? These are profound questions. We had better have something to eat while we consider them.

Erda's Earthy Chocolate Mousse

5 ounces bittersweet chocolate, chopped

5 egg yolks, beaten

5 egg whites, set aside

2 tbs. sugar

1 pinch of salt

1 cup heavy cream

2 tbs. kirschwasser

- In the bottom of a double boiler pot, bring some water to a boil, then lower to constant simmer.
- Place the chocolate in the top of the double boiler.

- Stir the chocolate occasionally until it is almost melted, then remove from heat and stir until smooth. Set aside to cool a bit.
- In a separate bowl, whip the cream to peak—whip it enough to be on the stiff side of creamy but not enough to become dry and mealy. Set aside.
- In another bowl, whip the egg whites with salt until soft peaks form. Sprinkle in the sugar and continue whipping to stiff peaks. Fold in the beaten egg yolks and the kirschwasser.
- Fold the melted chocolate into the egg and cream mixture. Fold, don't stir, until blended.
- Spoon the mousse into dessert cups and chill until firm. Allow at least an hour to refrigerate.
- Decorate with earthy-looking sprinkled toppings like shaved coconut, gummy worms, and crumbled chocolate wafer cookies.

Who cares if Erda has legs? Our palates are sated with the creamy chocolaty taste and Erda is still singing in her beautiful mezzo-soprano voice.

Erda warns, "*Give up the Ring, Wotan! A dark day for the gods is coming; all that is will end.*" Slowly she is swallowed up into the earth again. Wotan steps toward the fissure as if to follow Erda. "Wait!" he calls to her. He wants more of Erda's wisdom. But Fricka pulls him back and Wotan—finally and reluctantly—adds the Ring to the pile of gold for the giants.

Fafner starts packing up the gold. Fasolt tells him to be fair and calls on the gods to judge that the treasure is divided evenly. Loge confidentially advises Fasolt to let Fafner have all the treasure except for the Ring. So Fasolt attacks Fafner and takes the Ring. A struggle ensues. Fafner kills Fasolt, takes the Ring from his dead brother, throws it onto the pile, and calmly continues packing up.

The fratricide is played out to some fierce percussion:

The Fratricide

Fafner kills his brother Fasolt to get the powerful ring for himself. Arthur Rackham (1867-1939). Public domain.

After all that activity, Fafner must be hungry.

Giant Swedish Meatballs with Murder Sauce

1lb. ground beef

2 cups bread crumbs

1 cup stock, or 1 tbs. bouillon dissolved in 1 cup water

Oil for sautéing

1 egg lightly beaten

1 tsp. sugar

¼ tsp. allspice

¼ tsp. nutmeg

½ tsp. salt, more or less depending on how salty your stock or bouillon is

¼ tsp. pepper

½ cup heavy cream

- To make the crumbs, toast four slices of a hearty bread. Whir in the blender or chop finely. Set aside.
- Mix together all the ingredients except the ground beef, the bread crumbs, the bouillon, and the oil. Set aside. This is the cream sauce.
- In a separate bowl, add ½ cup bouillon to the bread crumbs. Stir until evenly moistened.
- Stir the ground beef into the bread crumbs until well mixed. Form into giant meatballs.
- Heat about 4 tablespoons of oil in a large skillet on low to medium heat. Place the meatballs in the skillet without crowding. Turning frequently, brown on all sides.
- Use tongs and a spoon to place the cooked meatballs in a baking dish.
- Pour the cream sauce into the skillet. Add the other ½ cup bouillon. Stir and cook on low heat until the sauce bubbles, about a minute.
- Pour the sauce over the meatballs and gently turn until they are evenly covered.

- Bake at 325° for about 30 minutes. You can test doneness by cutting a meatball and peeking inside to see the color, or use a thermometer to test. Beef is cooked when the inner temperature reaches 160°.
- Serve with the hottest, spiciest sauce you can find.

Giant Meatballs are pictured here with jalapeño, serrano, habanero, and Thai peppers, a favorite hot sauce of my family, and a tomato-base sauce for "blood."

With or without the murder sauce, the meatballs are delicious. Poor Fasolt missed out. Oh well, back to our story.

Wotan murmurs, "Whoa, that is some curse!" He is suddenly weighed down with worry and wonders if Erda, with her wisdom about the future, can advise him. He is sobered by his realization that he has paid for the construction of Valhalla with ill-gotten gains and we hear the Curse Motif once more. Fricka moves toward him and suggests that they all enjoy the comfort and shelter of their new home. Swinging his thunder-hammer, Donner clears the mist that has surrounded the fortress during this whole scene, and Froh shows the way over the Rainbow Bridge.

It is at this point that Wotan names their new home "Valhalla." Fricka asks what he means by Valhalla, as she has not heard the name before. Wotan never actually answers that question but cryptically responds that he has an idea and all will be revealed if it works out.

* * *

I'm going break from the narrative to clarify something that baffled me for a long time. Moments before this exchange, Wotan's words described Valhalla as being beautiful, lofty, and hard won. At this point, when he officially greets the fortress petitioning it to shelter the gods, we hear a solo trumpet playing the Sword Motif. At the same moment, Wotan's demeanor changes from worried to bold and decisive. These are clear indications that Wotan has an idea, but the idea itself is not revealed. We are left to wonder exactly what that idea is until the second act of *The Valkyrie*, when it is explained to us—sort of. But you don't have to wait; I am letting the cat out of the bag early. It should not be as cryptic as it is, and it would be unfortunate if you lost sleep tonight wondering about it.

As the gods are crossing the Rainbow Bridge to Valhalla, Wotan mutters some vaguely tuneful lines and then there is a trumpet fanfare, the simple Sword Motif:

Sword Motif

Wotan says, "Thus I salute the stronghold, safe from dread and dismay," and we hear the orchestrated Sword Motif. This triumphant fanfare, added to a reiteration of Erda's Motif, foretells a complicated plan. Wotan will descend to Erda to learn more about the fate of the world and his role in maintaining the *status quo* of the immortals' hierarchy. Since he needs protection for Valhalla, he will enlist Erda's help in creating a security force in the form of the Valkyries, their warrior daughters.

The second part of the idea, which is heralded by the Sword Motif, stems from Wotan's realization that, despite being the head honcho of the powerful godly elite, he cannot act as a free agent. He is, in fact, bound by the same power that he wields. He knows that he needs to get the Ring back from Fafner in order to keep it out of Alberich's hands and that ultimately it must be returned to the Rhine Maidens, but he cannot do this himself because of the contract with the giants. If he is to keep Valhalla, he must honor that contract. (Don't analyze this too carefully. Considering the scheming and thievery that he is involved in, it doesn't completely make sense that Wotan is suddenly worried about legalities. Wotan pretty much does what Wagner wants and *Wagner* is not bound by any of Wotan's contracts.)

Although it wasn't Wotan's intention, the Ring has become a part of the payment and he can't steal it away from Fafner. The contracts recorded in his spear, his marriage to Fricka, even his position as chief of the gods, combine to restrict his freedom to act as he deems necessary to save his reign. But what if there were a real free agent—a separate person, a Wotan-fearing human, a hero—who could kill Fafner and win the Ring back for Wotan? (The hero must be Wotan-fearing so he won't run off and keep the Ring for himself!) Wotan's plan is to create such a hero. His strategy involves living with the mortals on earth for a while in order to father this hero. Wotan will train him to be strong and fearless, while making the necessary arrangements in order to accomplish his goals. As we will see, the sword, infused with Wotan's magic, is an integral part of the plan, hence the distinctive Sword Motif rising out of Wotan's mumbled verses.

* * *

As the gods walk over the Rainbow Bridge, they can hear the Rhine Maidens pleading for their stolen gold to be returned. This is beautifully portrayed in the music, a slower, more somber variation on the Rhine Maidens' Joy in the Gold Motif.

Rhinegold Lament

Wotan tells Loge to make them stop their wailing. Loge yells to them that if they no longer have their gold's luster to enjoy, they can bask in the new-found splendor of the gods, by which he means they can enjoy the brilliance and majesty of Valhalla's reflection. The gods laugh, "Ha-ha-ha-ha," but the Rhine Maidens' voices continue lamenting and are the last we hear singing in the opera.

The work ends with a majestic march. Six harps depict the Rainbow Bridge, the undulating arpeggios of the string section illustrate the surging water in the Rhine River, and the brass section portrays the power and dignity of the gods.

Closing Scene of The Rhinegold, 1876, by Josef Hoffmann (1831-1904) . Public domain.

Time for a salad to clear our palates for *The Valkyrie*.

Rainbow Bridge Salad

- Cook 2-3 cups of rice. Wash and cut or slice different colored vegetables. Here are some suggestions:

Red Cabbage	Radicchio
Red Leaf Lettuce	Red Beets
Radishes	Tomatoes
Sweet Red Bell Peppers	Carrots
Orange Bell Peppers	Yellow Summer Squash
Yellow Bell Peppers	Peeled Cucumbers
Butter Lettuce	Romaine Lettuce
Green Bell Peppers	Arugula
Spinach	Purple Cabbage

- Over a bed of rice, arrange the vegetables in a rainbow design on a platter. The rice helps the vegetables stay in place.
- Splash with a vinaigrette dressing or place a small dish of dressing on the platter for dipping.
- Enjoy!

THE VALKYRIE

Act One

The opera opens with Siegmund running away from something. Onstage it is dark with flashes of light. The music indicates that there is a storm and we hear modifications of Wotan's Spear Motif woven through Donner's lightning and thunder music. The Spear Motif is a signal to the audience that Wotan is behind what is happening. The unfolding events are the result of Wotan's actions, not of random chance.

Donner's Motif

Spear Motif

Storm music, variations of the Spear Motif

etc.

Since we last saw Wotan promenading across the Rainbow Bridge to Valhalla, he has been very busy. (This is more thoroughly explained in long conversations during Act Two, but the story makes more sense if we know it now.) Recall that at the end of *The Rhinegold*, Wotan wanted Erda to stay a while to answer some questions. He urgently needed to know what she could tell him about the future. He wasn't able to find out all that Erda knew right then, but when the family was settled comfortably in Valhalla, Wotan took off to find Erda and hear her predictions.

The picture she painted for him was not rosy. "All things that are will end," she foretold, "A dark day dawns for the gods." Wotan and Erda spent many hours discussing how this might be prevented. They formulated ideas of protecting Valhalla and the structure of the godly hierarchy. What they finally developed was a way to enlist valiant, albeit dead, soldiers to guard Valhalla. Wotan and Erda had nine daughters, the Valkyries, who were part of this plan: the Valkyries would harvest dead heroes from battlefields, revive them, and bring them back to Valhalla to help protect it. We only hear about this; we do not see Erda again until the third act of *Siegfried*.

To fulfill another part of the plan, Wotan disguised himself as a mortal named Wälse (Wolf) and lived on earth with a mortal woman for a while. Mr. and Mrs. Wälse had children, a set of twins known as Siegmund and Sieglinde. Siegmund was to be the independent hero who would recapture the Ring from Fafner. Before the family fell apart (Siegmund will sing about that in a bit), Wälse told his son that in his darkest hour of need, he would find a sword that would get him out of trouble and carry him on to greatness.

Now, many years later, Siegmund is running through the woods during a storm. It is apparent that he is very tired. He comes across an unusual hut that it is built around a huge tree. Yes, there is a tree in the middle of the hut. Siegmund sings, "No matter whose home this is, I have to stop and rest." Sieglinde comes in, surprised to find a stranger in her house. Siegmund asks for something to drink and Sieglinde offers him water to quench his thirst.

Water

I guess we don't really need a recipe for water, but Sieglinde probably keeps some water with sliced cucumbers—and maybe a little sprig of mint—in a carafe in the fridge. It is very refreshing.

The storm music has faded into sweet lyrical passages played by the strings. Two lonely, unhappy people singing to each other with magnificent voices, are alone on the stage accompanied by a solo cello longing for fulfillment. Who wouldn't fall in love?

Sieglinde's Motif

Siegmund and Sieglinde chat for a little while. Sieglinde explains that "this house" and "this wife" belong to Hunding and says that Siegmund is welcome to stay. Custom demands that she extend hospitality and, besides, Sieglinde is curious about her guest. Siegmund lets her know that he is unarmed. His spear and shield were destroyed during a fight and he ran here while pursued by his enemies.

Sieglinde brings him a drinking horn filled with mead. Neither Wagner nor any of his commentators mention this, but Sieglinde keeps a batch of spiced mead warm in her crockpot. She leads a miserable life, without joy and with little hope. She has to have something to keep her going, so she probably stays tipsy most of the time. Surely, the mead deadens some of her pain.

Spiced Mead

3 cups mead
1 cinnamon stick, about 3 inches long
10 cloves
15 juniper berries

- In a crockpot or a pan over very low heat, stir the spices into the mead.
- Heat until just steaming. Some of the alcohol will evaporate if the mixture is allowed to boil.
- Let it brew on very low heat for an hour. Brewing allows the blend to develop a fullness of flavor.

For added authenticity, sip your mead from a drinking horn

Siegmund downs his mead and then gets up to go, saying he had better get on his way because he brings bad luck wherever he goes. Sieglinde replies that he cannot introduce bad luck where bad luck is a permanent resident. Intrigued, Siegmund changes his mind and decides to wait for Hunding to come home. Soon we hear the low brass announcing Hunding's arrival.

Scene Two

Hunding's Motif

Hunding is immediately suspicious, wondering who the stranger is and what he is doing in his house. Sieglinde explains that all she did was to give him something to drink because he was exhausted and had nowhere to rest.

Hunding declares that his home is sacred and that he hopes his hearth will be sacred to the visitor (in other words, don't take advantage of me). Then he orders Sieglinde to bring something to eat, so she goes into the kitchen and putters around for a couple minutes getting them some yummy soup to warm them up on a cold day in late winter.

Barley and Mushroom Soup

½ cup pearled barley (the box is sometimes labeled "quick barley")

1 ½ quarts water

2 bay leaves

2 tbs. butter

1 onion

1 pound mushrooms

1 rutabaga

4 carrots

1 tsp. vinegar

Salt and pepper to taste

- Put the water, bay leaves, and barley in a large soup pot or slow cooker and bring to a boil.
- Chop the onion.
- Melt the butter in a skillet and sauté the onion.
- While the onion is cooking, peel and chop the other vegetables and slice the mushrooms.
- When the water is boiling, add the onions, mushrooms, and vegetables to the barley. Cover the pot and lower the heat.
- Simmer for about an hour.
- Add the seasonings and vinegar. Serve hot.

While Sieglinde is getting supper ready, Hunding mumbles about his suspicions: he notices that the stranger has a very strong resemblance to his wife, and they both have a shifty, snake-like look about them.

Sieglinde brings the food and they sit down to eat. Hunding asks the stranger who he is and, rather than eating, Siegmund stands up and starts yakking away with his gorgeous *heldentenor* voice stating, "I am not Peaceful-man (*Friedmund*), I wish I could be Happy-man (*Frohwalt*), but unfortunately I am Woe-is-me-man (*Wehwalt*)." Then he goes on to tell them of his origins.

Long ago, he had a father a mother and a twin sister, the Wälsung, or Wolf, family. One day, while his father and he were out hunting, their home was ransacked. His mother was murdered and his sister disappeared. He and his father traipsed around the woods for a few years after that, hunting food and clashing with their enemies. Then, one day, his father disappeared during a skirmish. Siegmund searched and searched for his father, but all he ever found was a wolf skin. If we were in any doubt as to Siegmund's parentage, our doubt is dispelled by the orchestra playing the Valhalla Motif when Siegmund speaks of his father's disappearance. He was left alone and has been an outcast ever since. Everywhere he goes, he finds only woe.

Just today, he explains, he was wandering in the woods and found a forlorn young maiden who was being forced into a marriage with someone she didn't want to marry. She asked for Siegmund's protection. He protected her but, in the process, killed her two brothers. She was upset about her brothers' deaths and refused to leave their corpses. The brothers' kinsmen and neighbors arrived to avenge the situation. Siegmund continued to defend the maiden as long as he could, but his spear and shield were destroyed, the girl died, and everyone was on his trail, chasing him down.

He says, "So now you know, questioning woman, why I am not called *Friedmund*."

Peace Motif (This motif foreshadows deep human grief.)

At the end of Siegmund's explanation Hunding replies, "Aha! It was you who killed my friends!" Hunding is bound by the laws of hospitality to allow Siegmund to stay overnight but he vows that, in the morning, Siegmund will pay for the deaths that he has caused. "Defend yourself with strong weapons in the morning!"

Hunding then tells Sieglinde to prepare his bedtime drink. She busies herself in the kitchen once again. Before she takes the drink to Hunding, she looks at Siegmund in a meaningful way and then glances at the tree. Both her significant glance at the tree and the Sword Motif direct the audience's attention to the fact that there is a sword embedded in the trunk of the tree. She then goes into the bedroom to get Hunding out of the way by slipping him a mickey.

Hunding's Bedtime Sleepy Drink

4 tbs. (1–2 shots) B & B Liqueur or other fine brandy

½ cup cream

1 tbs. agave sweetener

¼ tsp. salt

1–2 squirts valerian herbal extract

- Mix all the ingredients together and heat until warm.

Scene Three

Siegmund remains in the main room of the hut, soliloquizing. He sings, "I'm really in a fix now. My father promised me that at the most perilous moment in my life, there would be a sword to help me out of danger."

 Get ready for a super-hero moment. Siegmund now sings the portion of *The Ring Cycle* that seems to have fostered an unofficial contest between *heldentenors* in various productions, who compete to hold the fermatas as long as possible. Try singing along when he calls to his father:

See what I mean about opera singers being super-heroes? The tenor can fill a huge theatre with his voice over dozens of *fortissimo* strings! And the suspense of that long note—whoa! That is a super-human power.

Then we hear a solo trumpet play the Sword Motif and, lo and behold, Siegmund sees the sword in the tree. He compares the glow of the sword to Sieglinde's shining gaze.

Sieglinde comes out from the bedroom and lets Siegmund know that he does not need to worry about Hunding for now because she has given him a sleeping draft. She tells Siegmund about her past and how the sword ended up in the trunk of the tree. When she was a child, she was kidnapped by villains who later gave her to Hunding and forced her to marry him. A strange one-eyed man in a floppy hat showed up in the middle of their wedding. He stuck a sword in the tree trunk and it is still there because no one has been able to pull it out. Her life has been so horrible that in order to survive and make each day bearable, she has held on to the hope that someday someone will show up who can pull the sword from the tree. She knows that person will be her salvation.

The music changes to sweet lyrical sounds. Siegmund and Sieglinde fall in love and sing the *Winterstürme* (Winter Storms) love song. "Winter's storms have yielded to the month of May" (literally, "the blissful moon"). They sing this mushy stuff for a while.

Winterstürme

They recognize each other as the fulfillment of dreamed-for soul mates. Siegmund says now that Sieglinde loves him, he no longer wants to be called Woe-is-me-man (*Wehwalt*); he receives the name he is known by: Victory-man. Sieglinde calls out his name, "Siegmund! So do I name you!"

Siegmund approaches the sword in the tree. He names it *Nothung,* or "Necessity," because he found it in his hour of need. He grasps the hilt singing, "Nothung! Nothung!" When he pulls it out of the tree, we hear the Sword Motif again. Triumphant, Siegmund claims Sieglinde as his wife. Sieglinde is ecstatic because she knows this is her true love; he is going to take her away from this horrible place and away from the horrible Hunding. While gazing at him and asking questions, she puts two and two together and realizes that Siegmund is her long-lost brother. She proclaims to him that, with his sword, he has won his own sister.

Although the audience may be creeped out by this initially, Wagner's idea is that the twins were incomplete without each other. Their union (or re-union) symbolizes the creation of a complete and perfect human, not quite divine but close to it, due to their paternity. In addition, this is the only way that Siegfried, the hero of the second half of the *Ring Cycle,* can be created with the genetic contribution of only one grandfather, Wotan. Act One ends with the twins hardly able to wait to get their clothes off.

The great Norwegian soprano, Kirsten Flagstad, as Sieglinde, 1935. (Photographer unknown.) Public domain.

Siegmund pulls Nothung from the Tree. Josef Hoffmann (1831-1904). Public domain.

Act Two

We are back on a rock in God-and-Goddess-Land with Wotan. We hear some really exciting music.

Scene One

It is Brünnhilde, Wotan's favorite Valkyrie daughter. Her cry, the cry of the Valkyries, "Hoyotoho!" is best translated as "Yee-hah!" or "Yippee!" All the noise and exciting music is Brünnhilde's fancy way of saying, "Hi, Dad!"

Cry of the Valkyries

Ho-jo-to-ho!   Ho-jo-to-ho!   He-ia-ha!   He-ia-ha!

Wotan gives Brünnhilde a heads-up that there will be a battle soon and instructs her to ensure victory for the Wälsung, Siegmund. As a warrior maiden, battle is her duty and she is happy to help out—she loves her work—but just now she hears a furious Fricka coming and she wants to get out of there. She doesn't like *this* kind of battle.

Fricka Approaches in Anger, 1910. Arthur Rackham (1867-1939). Public domain.

Fricka arrives in her chariot that is drawn by a team of rams. Surely, she keeps her goat population under control with delicious recipes like this:

Fricka's Goat Stew

¼ cup oil

2 onions

2 pounds goat meat

1 14-ounce can stewed tomatoes (or about 1 cup chopped fresh tomatoes)

3 red potatoes

4 carrots

1 parsnip

1 quart water, chicken broth, or bouillon

½ cup flour

½ tsp. garlic salt (or a few cloves of garlic)

Dash of cinnamon (or, better, throw a cinnamon stick in the pot)

Dash of cayenne pepper

Salt and pepper to taste

- Chop the onions, cube the vegetables, and peel and cut the meat into stew-sized cubes removing as much of the bone as you can.
- Heat the oil in a Dutch oven or soup pot.
- Cook the chopped onions in the oil until translucent.
- Mix the flour and spices together, then dredge the meat in the flour until well coated.
- Add the meat to the onions and brown in the hot oil.
- Stir in the remaining ingredients and bring to a boil.
- Lower the heat, cover, and simmer for about 1½ hours, stirring occasionally.
- Remove the cover and continue cooking another ½ hour until the meat is tender and the sauce is thickened. Remove the cinnamon stick and garlic cloves.
- Garnish with chopped dried apricots and parsley or cilantro.
- Serve over rice or with a hearty bread.

Goat Stew garnished with chopped dried apricots

This part of the opera doesn't have a lot of action, but the discussion between Fricka and Wotan is important to note. Fricka sings of the pain caused by years of Wotan's infidelity and of the torment he is continuing to inflict on her by protecting Siegmund, one of the products of his philandering. She is especially ticked off about the brother-sister incest thing.

Wotan is in a little bit of a quandary because, although he risked one of his eyes in order to win Fricka's hand in marriage and to acquire her wisdom, he now finds that wisdom inconvenient. Fricka's particular area of knowledge, that of customs, law, and order, was instrumental in helping Wotan to achieve his powerful position as chief of the gods. Wotan knows he can't have a structured society without some laws, but occasionally he finds these laws to be problematic. Fricka points out that Wotan has completely disparaged the laws of marriage and incest by setting up the events of Act One. To add insult to injury, he is flaunting the transgression of her laws by protecting Siegmund now. It is humiliating.

Wotan replies, "Even after all these years, you still don't get it. You hang on to tradition, the conventional ideas of the past, and all your laws. What is needed is a mortal who is a free agent and does what must be done: that which is unlawful for the gods to do." Wotan *must* get that Ring back! He argues that Siegmund is his own man, an independent hero.

Fricka thinks, "Um, hello?" and points out some inconsistencies in Wotan's logic. Did Siegmund just happen to run to the hut where Sieglinde lived and did he just happen to find the sword that Wotan just happened to leave in a certain tree? Fricka just doesn't accept that Siegmund is an independent agent. Wotan had a meddling hand throughout Siegmund's life, from his childhood to these recent events. If Siegmund is so free from Wotan's influence, then Wotan should take away the sword that is infused with divine power. Fricka's other complaint is that Hunding was wronged when Sieglinde was stolen from him. Theirs was a legal marriage; whether anybody was happy or not is beside the point. Hunding has the right to avenge the offense in a fair fight, not in a battle against a magic sword.

Wotan knows that Fricka is right. He understands that his reign relies on laws that give a structure to society and by his compliance with the terms of the contracts that are inscribed on his spear. One of those contracts is surely the marriage agreement between Fricka and himself, in which he agreed to love and honor her. Slowly, Wotan gives in to Fricka's line of reasoning: because of his transgression, Siegmund must face Hunding in battle. It must be a fair battle (basically so that Hunding can kill Siegmund and exact revenge). Fricka insists that Wotan must not protect Siegmund and that Wotan and Brünnhilde must, instead, defend Fricka's honor.

Wotan has lost the argument. His elaborate plan to get the Ring back failed. He reluctantly agrees that in order to maintain world order, with the gods in their place at the top, *he* must adhere to social rules and therefore relinquish his protection of Siegmund. As Fricka is summing up, we can hear Brünnhilde hoyotoho-ing offstage, ready to rejoin her dad. She enters the stage, passing Fricka, who is on her way out.

Fritz Feinhals (1869-1940) as Wotan, 1903. (Photo by Ad. Baumann, Munich.) Public domain.

Scene Two

Brünnhilde now has a very long heart-to-heart with Wotan. (Many people sleep through this part because it's just monologues and conversation without action. I'll let you know when to wake up.)

Wotan's soliloquy is a recapitulation of what has taken place so far in the cycle. He explains to Brünnhilde what we already know from the spoilers mentioned at the end of *The Rhinegold* and earlier in this chapter: that the Valkyries were created by Wotan and Erda to avert Erda's prediction about the end of the world. He goes on to explain that, in order to maintain his hierarchy, he must make sure that Alberich does not get the Ring back; Wotan *must* have it. But he cannot grab it himself because he must abide by the contracts on his spear. He needs an agent, Siegmund, to get it from Fafner, who has taken the form of a dragon and protects the treasure in a cave in the East. We also learn that another of Erda's predictions has come to pass: Alberich has fathered an evil son whose sole ambition is to obtain the Ring.

Wait. What? Alberich has a son? (Be patient, we'll talk about that during *Twilight of the Gods*.)

Wotan placed many dangers and obstacles in Siegmund's path in order to help him become the hoped-for independent and fearless hero who could brave the dragon to get the Ring back. But Siegmund is not independent after all, having been conceived and pretty much formed by Wotan. Neither father nor son can accomplish the goals that were set out by Wotan in order to put the world back on its course. "I, who am master through treaties, to my own treaties am now a slave!" complains Wotan.

The part of the discussion that has immediate importance to our story is Wotan's command to Brünnhilde that she is not to protect Siegmund after all. She must let Hunding fight Siegmund, and Siegmund must fight without the sword Nothung and without her help. Brünnhilde argues with Wotan because she knows that, in his heart, he loves Siegmund and his true wish is for Siegmund to be protected. Brünnhilde says that she is only an extension of her father, of Wotan's will. She knows that his genuine desire is for her to protect Siegmund. He must live so that he can fulfill the destiny that Wotan has planned for him. Wotan insists that Brünnhilde *must not* protect Siegmund. After he storms off the stage, she very reluctantly admits that she must forsake Siegmund.

Scene Three

Scene Three opens with more running. This time Siegmund and Sieglinde are running away from Hunding. They are exhausted and they have to rest and eat something. They need to rehydrate and get some energy from the dried food they wisely packed to bring along.

Electrolyte Water

1 quart water
½ tsp. baking soda
½ tsp. salt
2 tbs. honey or corn syrup
1 tbs. lemon juice

- Combine all the ingredients in a water bottle and sip during your workout, or while running away from dangerous Vikings. Refrigerate unused portion.

Beef Jerky

1 pound very thinly sliced top round steak
½ cup brown sugar
1½ cups water
½ cup soy sauce
½ cup vegetable oil

- Combine the sugar and water in a large shallow bowl or casserole dish. Stir until the sugar is dissolved.
- Add soy sauce and oil, mix well.
- Add the steak slices.
- Marinate overnight in the refrigerator.
- Heat the oven to 200°. (If you have a food dehydrator, ignore the rest of this recipe and follow the manufacturer's instructions.)
- Lay the steak slices on the slotted top of a broiler pan. The bottom of the broiler pan will collect the excess marinade that drips off. Dry in oven at 200° for 8-10 hours until the meat is ready.
- Store in an airtight container. If you don't eat it right away, keep it in the refrigerator.

After her snack, Sieglinde hears the hunting horns and hounds. She has a prophetic vision in which the ash tree splits and topples. She collapses into Siegmund's' arms.

Scene Four

Sieglinde sleeps but we are awake (yes, it is time to wake up) to hear the Fate Motif, which begins Scene Four.

Fate Motif

Brünnhilde shows up and greets Siegmund. Siegmund asks, "Who are you?" She explains that only those who are about to die can see her. It's going to be great because after he dies, she will put him on her horse and take him to Valhalla where he'll join all the other fallen war heroes and protect the gods' fortress. He'll even be able to see his father, Wälse. Death: it's a great life!

Siegmund asks a series of questions. When he finds out that Sieglinde cannot come with him, he rejects Brünnhilde's summons. He says, "No. If Sieglinde can't come with me then I'm not going. We would both be insufferably lost and miserable, not to mention sad, without each other." So if he has to die anyway, first he is going to kill Sieglinde and then kill himself. That way, even if they are in hell, they can be together. He is ready to follow through with this, demonstrating to Brünnhilde his commitment and the deep love he has for Sieglinde. Brünnhilde has never seen anything quite like this, which moves her very deeply. So, contrary to what she's been told to do by Wotan, she makes her own decision and says, "Okay, never mind; I'll help you. I shall change the course of the battle so that you and Sieglinde can continue to live."

Brünnhilde retreats to wait for the battle to begin.

Lillian Nordica (1857 – 1914) *as Brünnhilde*, 1898.   (Photo by Aimé Dupont 1842–1900.) Public domain.

Scene Five

Sieglinde is sleeping and Siegmund sings of his love for her. Horns announce that Hunding is on his way. Siegmund, trusting in his divinely-powered sword, jumps up for battle. Just as Brünnhilde is going to step in and protect him, Wotan arrives and shoos Brünnhilde away so she cannot protect Siegmund. Nothung is shattered and, in the ensuing battle, Hunding kills Siegmund.

At the end of Act Two it is interesting to know a little about the motifs that Wagner included. After Sieglinde wakes up, we hear Hunding's Motif. Then there is a storm theme, that same stormy thunder and lightning we heard in the beginning of this opera. Then we can hear the Sword Motif during the battle. We hear the Valkyrie theme when Brünnhilde shows up. Then we hear the Spear Motif when Wotan enters the fray and then the Fate Motif after Hunding kills Siegmund. So even if you aren't watching the stage, or can't see the action because of the mist that Wagner ordered, you can figure out what is happening by the *leitmotifs*, or themes, you hear in the music. The music is brilliant.

After Siegmund dies, Brünnhilde gathers up the shards of Nothung, grabs Sieglinde, and zips away. Wotan kneels beside Siegmund and we witness his deep sorrow in losing his son. This is the hero that he had pinned all of his hopes on. He was meant to have saved the world as Wotan knew it—the world in which every population had a position and a rank: the giants in one place, the Nibelungs in another, the humans in their place, and the gods in charge. The only way that Wotan could retain the stability of this order was to get the Ring back from Fafner and put it back where it belonged: in the Rhine under the protection of the Rhine Maidens. But, as powerful as he is, this is something he cannot do. An independent hero, a human who was brave beyond measure and not influenced by other forces, was needed to do this action so that Wotan could remain true to the contracts he had made. So much for that plan.

Wotan is looking mournfully at Siegmund's dead body. Here lies his favorite son, and this dumb cluck Hunding has killed him. Wotan snarls at Hunding to "kneel before Fricka," and waves his hand, causing Hunding to fall down dead.

Well, that's enough grieving. Wotan erupts in rage against Brünnhilde, "the criminal" who disobeyed him. Act Two ends with Wotan exiting the stage to thunder and lightning depicted by amazingly powerful music.

Act Three

Scene One

Act Three begins with the most famous part of *The Ring* and possibly the most well-known of Wagner's music: the Ride of the Valkyries. Eight Valkyries ride onto the stage, each with a dead hero thrown over the back of her horse. They cry "Hoyotoho!" to each other as a greeting because they enjoy their job and they are having a grand old time.

Valkyrie Motif

Wagner's original idea for this act was to have real horses on the stage. The production with live horses onstage didn't exactly go smoothly. It took some of the drama away from the story because audiences were distracted by what the horses were doing; evidently horses are not good actors. It is my understanding that real horses have not been used for a long time. But, inspired by horses, this recipe is in honor of Wagner's original idea. The horses would want a snack, too.

Amalia Materna as Brünnhilde with Cocotte as Grane, from the first Bayreuth production of *Die Walküre*, 1876.
(Photo by Joseph Albert, 1825-1886). Public domain.

Grane's Oats and Carrot Bars

1 cup regular oats

½ cup milk

1 8-ounce can crushed pineapple

2 eggs

¼ cup vegetable oil

1 tsp. vanilla extract

1½ cups flour

1 cup brown sugar

1 tbs. baking powder

½ tsp. baking soda

1 tsp. cinnamon

½ tsp. ground ginger

½ tsp. salt

1½ cups shredded carrots (about 6 carrots)

½ cup golden raisins

- Preheat the oven to 350°.
- Combine the oats with the milk and let stand for a few minutes while the oats soften.
- Break the eggs into a small bowl and beat lightly to mix the yolk and white together.
- Add the eggs, canned pineapple (and juice—do not drain), oil, and vanilla.
- Mix well.
- In a separate bowl, combine the flour, sugar, baking powder, baking soda, cinnamon, ginger, and salt.
- Stir in the grated carrots and raisins.
- Add the egg and oats mixture to the dry ingredients.
- Mix together gently until all dry ingredients are moistened.
- If your batter is too thick, add applesauce or apple butter.

- For bars, bake in an oiled and flour-dusted 8" x 8" baking pan for 40 minutes. For a loaf that can be sliced, bake in a prepared 9" x 4" loaf pan for 50-60 minutes. Batter is done when a toothpick inserted in the center is removed clean.
- Slice or cut into bars when cool.

Once the Valkyries are done laughing and greeting each other, they notice there are only eight of them. Where is Brünnhilde? One of them looks up and says, "Here she comes! That's strange, there isn't a dead warrior on her horse with her. It is a live woman!" Brünnhilde reins in her horse, Grane, and asks her sisters for protection. She tells them that she has done something about which Wotan is a bit unhappy.

When Sieglinde gets a chance to speak, she says something on the order of, "It's very kind of you to take so much trouble for little ol' me, but I don't want to continue living without Siegmund. Life without him is going to be torture for me so, please, just kill me now." The music Sieglinde sings is intensely plaintive and heart-wrenching.

However, Brünnhilde has an announcement that will change Sieglinde's mind. She brightens the somber mood by singing a triumphant passage announcing that Sieglinde is pregnant—and not just ordinarily pregnant; she will give birth to the greatest hero the world has ever known. The hero will redeem the world with the help of Nothung, the sword. Brünnhilde gives the shattered pieces of Nothung to Sieglinde and tells her to save them for her son. The hero will put things back on their proper course and his name will be Siegfried. Sieglinde answers Brünnhilde with the Redemption Motif, "O most noble wonder, glorious maiden!" This music is so beautiful it just knocks your socks off.

Redemption Motif

We hear rumbling in the distance. Wotan is on his way. The Valkyries tell Sieglinde to run away and hide in the East because Wotan avoids going over there, near the dragon. Sieglinde runs away to hide from Wotan and to give birth safely to her hero child.

This is the last time we see Sieglinde and it's too bad because she always has such an incredible voice to sing that beautiful music. But on with the story.

Onstage now, there are nine Valkyries screaming, screeching, and trembling because they can hear Wotan coming.

Scene Two

From offstage Wotan starts bellowing "Where is Brünnhilde? Where is the criminal?" Brünnhilde is hiding behind her eight sisters. Wotan calls his daughters cowards; he is upset with all the Valkyries because he didn't train them to act like fraidy-cats, but, yikes, Wotan is scary when he is angry! Finally Brünnhilde comes out and faces Wotan.

By disobeying him, she has dishonored him and she must be punished. The rest of the Valkyries are screaming, "No, no!" in the background, but he continues to outline the punishment. Brünnhilde will be banished, her divinity revoked, and her lot will be that of any medieval mortal woman: wife to a domineering husband. Wotan warns the other Valkyries to get the heck out of his sight if they don't want to share her fate. They flee.

The Ride of the Valkyr, by John Charles Dollman (1851-1934). (Illustration from the book *Myths of the Norsemen from the Eddas and Sagas*, by Helene Adeline Guerber, 1909.) Public domain.

Scene Three

After the eight noisy Valkyries leave, Wotan and Brünnhilde engage in a passionate discussion about her fateful decision and what will happen to her. Brünnhilde's punishment is to be placed into a magic sleep on top of a rocky cliff and left there to be rescued (or, rather, claimed) by the first guy who wanders by. She will have to be his wife and servant. Brünnhilde is contrite, but at the same time a bit indignant. She says that she only did what she knew was Wotan's true desire. "After all," she says, "I am only an extension of your will. That's my whole reason for being: to carry out your wishes. Only *I* knew your true feelings for Siegmund, no matter what you had agreed to with Fricka." This does not matter to Wotan because she disobeyed a direct order.

Brünnhilde, ultimately, is resigned to her fate, but pleads with Wotan to at least put some sort of barrier between her and the world so that she won't end up with some plebian chump. As a former member of his household, that fate would bring shame to Wotan and the other Valkyries, too.

This has been a pretty bad day for Wotan: he lost an argument with Fricka, saw his son Siegmund die, watched his elaborate plans fail, and now he has to banish his favorite daughter. Eventually he agrees to surround Brünnhilde with a ring of fire. That way, only a hero who has never experienced fear, and therefore doesn't know that he should be afraid of fire, will actually have the courage to go through the fire to find Brünnhilde. Being the wife of a very courageous hero would be more dignified for a former member of Wotan's household. It would be less shameful for everyone involved. Saving face is a big deal for these characters.

Brünnhilde is put under a magic spell and falls asleep.

Magic Sleep Motif

Magic Fire Motif

Wotan kisses away her godhood and covers her with her armor. He sings a heart-rending piece about his love for Brünnhilde and then summons Loge to start the fire that will surround her. The orchestra plays Loge's music, the Magic Fire Motif. As the fire gains power, several other leitmotifs enter the music, including a very slow version of Siegfried's Motif, to which Wotan sings, "He who fears my spear's point, shall never pass through the fire."

Siegfried's Motif variation

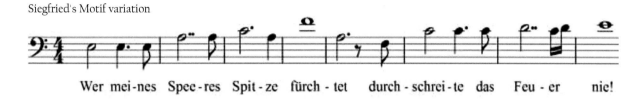

Wer mei-nes Spee-res Spit-ze fürch-tet durch-schrei-te das Feu-er nie!

Wotan and the Valkyrie Brunhild, 1892, by Konrad Dielitz (1845-1933). Public domain.

Does this make you hungry? It's time for dinner and the cooking fire is ready—Brünnhilde won't care, she is asleep. This time let's make something for the Valkyries, like chicken...

Valkyrie Candy-Curried Chicken Wings

10-12 chicken wings or 20-24 drumettes

1 onion

3 cloves garlic

2 tsp. salt

2 tsp. turmeric

1 tbs. ground cumin

1 tbs. ground coriander

1 tbs. ground ginger

1 tbs. onion powder

1 tsp. garlic powder, or more if you like

Dash to ¼ tsp. cayenne pepper, depending on your spiciness preference

½ cup to 1 cup olive oil (enough to cover the chicken while marinating)

½ cup little cinnamon candies: about 4 oz. Cinnamon Imperials, sold as bagged candy or cake decorations. (Red Hots, or diced Hot Tamales candies can also be used but they don't dissolve as quickly.)

- Clean the chicken and place in large, shallow dish for marinating.
- Peel and chop the onion and the garlic.
- Whisk all the spices and the candies together with the oil in a skillet. Add the onion and garlic.
- Cook on low heat until the onion is translucent and the candy begins to dissolve, 10-15 minutes.
- Pour the spicy oil over the chicken, making sure all the pieces are covered.
- Marinate several hours or overnight.
- Cook over a gas or charcoal grill about 15-20 minutes, turn and grill another 15 minutes until done.

Spicy, sweet, yummy!

SIEGFRIED

Act One

Siegfried opens with mysterious music, featuring the Brooding Motif, that illustrates the thoughts of Mime, the Nibelung, who now lives as a blacksmith in a shabby hut in the woods.

Brooding Motif

When the curtain rises, Mime is hammering a sword on an anvil. He sings about all the work he has done trying to forge a sword for Siegfried. The swords could serve a giant but Siegfried manages to break every one with the first strike. He sings about Nothung: if he could fix *that* sword, Siegfried could use it to kill Fafner. With Fafner out of the way, Mime would be closer to getting possession of the Ring. But there is something about the pieces of Nothung that will not allow Mime to smelt them. We now know that the broken pieces of Nothung collected by Brünnhilde (at the end of Act Two of *The Valkyrie*) have made their way to this little hut where Mime lives. Mime continues to complain and hammer until the sword is finished. At that point, Siegfried enters singing "Hi-ho!"

Hoi - ho!

He wears primitive clothing and has a hunting horn slung from his belt. He escorts a bear into the hut saying that the bear is better company then Mime has ever been. Understandably, Mime is frightened. Calm down, Mime, have a bear claw.

Siegfried's Hazelnut Bear Claws

This recipe has six elements: dough, filling, nut topping, glaze, icing, and slivered almond "claws."

Ingredients you will need:

Frozen puff pastry sheets

½ cup finely chopped hazelnuts

2 tsp. hazelnut extract

Slivered almonds, 24–40 pieces

1 egg

2 tbs. milk + 1 tbs. milk

2 tbs. butter

1½ cups panko or fine bread crumbs

2 tbs. granulated sugar + ½ cup granulated sugar + 1 cup powdered sugar

1 tbs. corn syrup

¼ cup water

Baking sheet or jelly roll pan

Pastry brush

Step one, prepare the dough and the nut toppings.
- Thaw the frozen dough overnight in the refrigerator.
- Chop the hazelnuts.
- Choose four slivered almonds per "paw," ones that look most like claws. Set aside until the end.

Step two, prepare the filling:

2 tbs. butter

1 egg

2 tbs. granulated sugar

2 tsp. hazelnut extract

1 cup panko or fine bread crumbs

2 tbs. milk
- Melt the butter, set aside.
- Break the egg into a small dish or ramekin, whisk. Pour about half into a larger bowl, reserving the rest for later.
- Add melted butter, sugar, hazelnut extract, and panko to the larger bowl; stir well.
- Whisk the milk into the reserved egg and set aside.

Step three, assemble and bake the paws:
- Heat oven to 350°.
- Prepare the baking sheet by lining with parchment paper.
- The frozen pastry dough comes in two folded pieces. One piece at a time, roll the dough into large rectangles, about 10" by 15".
- Using ½ the filling for each piece, place filling lengthwise down the center third of each pastry rectangle.
- Fold the dough by rolling ⅓ over the filling lengthwise, then folding again over the last ⅓ so that the seam is on the bottom.
- Very gently, flatten about an inch of the rolled pastry along one side. (This side will be the "toes" of the bear's paw.)

- Cut the dough into pieces: three pieces for bear-sized pastries, five for daintier teddy-bear claws.
- Make three 1'' cuts along the flattened edge of each piece of dough for the toes.
- Find the egg and milk mixture, whisk again.
- Brush the top of each pastry with the egg and milk mixture.
- Sprinkle the chopped nuts over the top. You may have to press them gently into the dough if they won't stick.
- Place the pastries on the parchment paper and arrange so the toes are spread apart to look like bear paws.
- Bake about 25-30 minutes, until golden brown.
- Remove baking sheet from oven and place it on a cooling rack. Leave the pastries on the parchment paper until the glaze and icing have been added.

Step four, prepare the glaze:

½ cup granulated sugar

¼ cup water

1 tbs. corn syrup

- Mix the glaze ingredients in a small saucepan
- Heat to a full boil, remove from heat, and set aside to cool.
- When the pastries have cooled about five minutes, drizzle a little cooled glaze over each one.

Step five, prepare icing:

1 cup powdered sugar

1 tbs. milk

- Place the powdered sugar in a bowl.
- Add the milk by ¼ teaspoons, mixing until you have a good consistency. The icing should be thin enough to drip from a spoon, but still thick and white. If it is too thin, it will soak into the pastry just like the glaze.
- When the pastries are completely cooled, drip some icing over each one.

Step six, *decorate.*

- *To make the claws, carefully push a slivered almond into the top of each toe.*

After eating one of these scrumptious pastries, Mime tells Siegfried he has another sword for him to try. Siegfried lets the bear go back into the woods. He picks up the new sword, strikes it against the anvil, and the sword breaks. Siegfried explodes in a tirade. Hoping to appease him, Mime offers Siegfried some roast meat and soup. Siegfried says, "Oh yuck! I don't want your slop. I gag on the food you prepare."

Mime's Soup

Ew, never mind. We'll take Siegfried's reaction to Mime's offer as a forewarning not to include any recipes from Mime.

Siegfried is not at all nice to Mime. He complains that Mime disgusts him and the only reason he comes back home to Mime is to find out the truth about his heritage. *"Who are my father and mother?"* he demands of the dwarf. When he grabs Mime by the throat and threatens to strangle him, Mime finally comes clean and tells Siegfried the story of his birth.

Mime tells his story singing to his Sob Story Motif:

Mime's Mission, also called the Sob Story Motif

Years ago, Mime found a suffering woman in the woods. It was Sieglinde, who was in labor. He took her in and cared for her but, although her baby was born alive, Sieglinde died. Before her death, however, she left instructions that the child was to be called Siegfried and she mentioned that the father was killed in battle. Siegfried wants proof from Mime that this story is true, so Mime shows him the broken pieces of Nothung. Siegfried is liberated by this information. He claims Nothung as his birthright and says he can now go forth into the world without ever having to see the hated Mime again.

Throughout his entire childhood, Siegfried was essentially kept prisoner by Mime. Contrary to Mime's narrative, which describes a loving home and caring guidance, Mime actually ignored Siegfried and only gave him enough food, clothing, and shelter to survive. Siegfried gripes that he only learned to talk because he forced Mime to teach him. After delivering a few more blows to Mime, Siegfried commands him to make the sword immediately. He bounds out into the woods, hoping that when he gets back he'll have his own sword and he will be able to leave Mime forever.

Siegfried's behavior toward Mime in this scene is quite violent; whether or not the brutality is enacted by the actors, the orchestra leaves the audience in no doubt about the violent nature of the relationship by means of many sudden, sharp passages in the music. Herculean Siegfried *is* physically abusive to dwarfish Mime, however Mime is not an innocent victim. He came up from Nibelheim and prowled around until he found Sieglinde and he raised Siegfried with one intention: to possess the Ring. He fantasizes that Siegfried will kill Fafner the dragon and once

Fafner is dead, Mime will get rid of Siegfried and have the treasure all to himself. So lest we start feeling any sympathy for Mime, we need to remember that the only reason he took care of Siegfried was in order to get possession of the Ring—there was no altruism or kindness involved in his actions.

After Siegfried's departure, Mime wonders how he will lure Siegfried to Fafner, and how he will ever get the shards of the sword to become whole again. He is immersed in contemplation in order to find answers to these difficulties. The last thing he wants at this point is to be interrupted. His music,

Mime's Frustration, also considered a variation of the Lovelessness Motif

is accompanied by the orchestra with traces of the Curse Motif and the Dragon's Motif and morphs into a stately chord progression, which ushers in the next scene.

Scene Two

Wanderer Motif

A guest, wearing a floppy old hat, an overcoat, a patch over one eye and carrying a spear, arrives. This, by the way, is the same description of the stranger who showed up at Sieglinde's wedding. Mime makes it clear that he does not want any company, but the guest intrudes and introduces himself by saying, "The world calls me Wanderer."

Wand' - rer,   heisst   mich   die   Welt.

65

The eye patch and Spear Motif identify Wanderer as Wotan. Wotan has abandoned his comfortable home, Valhalla, and his duties as chief god. He has been wandering around looking for a way to redeem the world that he used to govern. Evidently he has also abandoned the Golden Apples, because he is aging.

Against Mime's wishes, Wanderer enters the hut and sits at the hearth. Mime is wary of the stranger and does not recognize him as Wotan. All he wants is for Wanderer to go away. As a Nibelung, Mime has no respect for human customs and ignores the laws of hospitality. If he were a better host, he would have offered Wanderer some hot tea and invited him to rinse his weary feet in a basin of refreshing lemon-scented warm water.

Chai Latte

2 cups water

1 cinnamon stick

12 cardamom pods or 1½ tsp. ground cardamom

2 cloves

8 peppercorns

1 to 2 tbs. sugar

1 cup milk

Darjeeling tea: 1½ tbs. loose tea or 3 teabags

- Grind the cardamom seeds, cloves, and pepper with a mortar and pestle.
- Combine the water, cinnamon, and ground spices together in a sauce pan. Bring to a boil.
- Cover, lower the heat, and simmer for at least 10 minutes. If the cardamom seeds are not finely ground, allow to simmer 20-30 minutes.
- When the spices are very fragrant, add the milk and sugar. Bring to a simmer again.
- Sprinkle the loose tea over the liquid, or add the teabags.
- Cover and turn off the heat.
- Steep for 4 to 5 minutes.
- Strain the tea into cups and serve immediately. Makes enough for two mugs.

Refreshing Foot Soak

2 cups rock salt

1 tsp. lemon extract

2 cups Epsom salts

1 cup baking soda

1 cup mint leaves or ¼ cup dried mint

1 lemon

- If you are using fresh mint, spread the leaves on a baking sheet and dry the mint in the oven at 250° for 20-30 minutes.
- Cut the lemon into very thin slices.
- Place on a rack in the oven at 250° for about 2 hours.
- Put the rock salt in a jar and add the lemon extract.
- Cover the jar and shake well to mix the lemon fragrance into the salt.
- Add the Epsom salts and baking soda to the jar. Shake well.
- Add the lemon slices and mint to the jar and shake again.
- Allow the mixture to rest for 24 hours before using so that the fragrances infuse nicely.
- Store the Foot Soak in a cool dry place or, better, refrigerate.
- To use, add about a cup of the mixture to a small tub of hot water. Sprinkling a few rose petals over the surface makes it pretty and adds more color. You can soak your feet while enjoying a mug of chai.

While Wanderer is resting, he invites Mime to ask him whatever he needs to know. Mime resists, repeating that Wanderer should just go away, but Wanderer is persistent. He has traveled the world and knows about many things. Mime must ask three questions and if he doesn't get a satisfactory answer to any of the questions, he may have Wanderer's head. This question-and-answer game is Wagner's way of reviewing the events of the story, as he does in each opera of the cycle.

Mime sticks to what he considers safe subjects, asking questions to which he already knows the answers. His first question is, "Who lives in the depths, under the earth?" Wanderer answers, "The Nibelungs. At one time, they were slaves of Black Alberich, the Nibelung who amassed a great treasure."

Mime asks, "Who lives on the surface of the earth?" "The earth's surface is the domain of the Giants," answers Wanderer and he expands by relating the story of the treasure and the murder of Fasolt.

Mime's third question is, "Who lives up in the clouds?" Wanderer's answer is, "In the cloudy heights, the gods reside in Valhalla. Light Alberich, Wotan, rules there." Hang on a second. Wotan has just referred to himself as "Light Alberich," as if in contrast to mentioning "Black Alberich" several lines earlier. This is rather mysterious. Has Wotan come to the realization that the lust for power makes him Alberich's parallel? Rather than being opposites of each other, are they in actuality counterparts?

Anton van Rooy as The Wanderer, from a 1906 production of *Siegfried*. (Photo by Studio Aimé Dupont, New York.) Public domain.

Wanderer then takes a turn asking Mime questions, with Mime's head as the wager. "Who are the humans most favored by Wotan?" Mime answers correctly that the Wälsung lineage was well-loved—and ill-treated—by Wotan. Siegmund and Sieglinde were the parents of the strongest of the Wälsungs, Siegfried.

Before Wanderer asks his next question, he lets Mime know that he is wise to his intentions. "A Nibelung raised Siegfried as a means to kill Fafner and get the Ring and the hoard. What is the name of the sword that Siegfried must use to kill Fafner?" By this time, Mime is absorbed in the game and notices nothing fishy about this leading question. Mime knows that the answer is "Nothung" and he excitedly discloses this information to Wanderer, also relating some of Nothung's history. Wanderer's first two questions have increased Mime's confidence and, distracted, he has relaxed a bit. This assurance, however, is short-lived.

Wanderer's last question, "Who will be able to forge Nothung from the sword's fragments?" sends Mime into a tizzy. Of course Mime cannot answer that; he has been struggling with those fragments for years. Wanderer reproves Mime, asserting that he should have used the opportunity to gather information he needed, instead of asking unimportant questions to which he already knows the answers. Wanderer then says that only someone who has never known fear will be able to forge Nothung and he bequeaths Mime's head to that fearless person: ". . . I leave your wise head to the one who has not learned fear." Wotan lets us know who that is, if we hadn't guessed already, by singing these words to Siegfried's Motif.

ver - fal-len   lass' ich es dem,   der das Furch-ten   nicht   ge - lernt!

Wanderer's guessing game is Wotan's roundabout way of sanctioning Siegfried's execution of Mime. Finally, having achieved the purpose of his visit—a sort of legal authorization for Siegfried to kill Mime—Wanderer wanders off.

Scene Three

Siegfried rushes back to the hut demanding his new sword. Mime answers that he hasn't finished it because he has been contemplating a weighty matter. He is reluctant to let Siegfried go out into the world without understanding the meaning of fear, something he has neglected to teach him. Siegfried does not understand what he means, so he describes fear as hammering of the heart, shuddering, quaking, and quivering. Siegfried wants to know more about this fear thing; it sounds like fun. Mime suggests that they go together to Fafner's cave, where the dragon certainly will teach Siegfried about fear. But Siegfried wants his sword first.

Mime admits failure in repairing Nothung, so Siegfried grabs the pieces and says he'll just forge the sword himself. Here is some really terrific music, including three new motifs:

The Labor Motif, while Siegfried is filing the shards of the broken sword

The Bellows Motif, during the smelting phase

The Hammering Motif, during which Siegfried provides the percussion while he reshapes Nothung

During Siegfried's smelting and hammering songs, Mime comes up with a plan to get rid of Siegfried. Scurrying around the hut and mumbling to himself, he concocts a strong potion to give to Siegfried once the dragon is dead. Mime rejoices in his plan. He will offer Siegfried a drink to quench his thirst after the battle with Fafner. Just a few drops of the potion and Siegfried will conk out, giving Mime the opportunity to kill Siegfried with his own sword. Mime's scheming comments weave through Siegfried's bellows and forging songs.

Mime's Swift-Acting Sleeping Potion

No recipe here; I don't want you to get sick. Anyway, it has already been established that Mime was a bad cook.

Siegfried strikes his new sword against the anvil to test it as he has done for the swords that Mime made for him previously. Instead of the sword shattering, the *anvil* breaks in two!

Siegfried Forges Balmung by Howard Pyle (1853-1911). (Illustration from *The Story of Siegfried* by James Baldwin, 1882.)
Public domain. [Balmung is the sword's name from Norse mythology.]

Act Two

Prelude

It is dark, so we can't see much. The mysterious low-brass music lets us know we are in the dark woods near Fafner's cave.

Scene One

When the curtain rises, Alberich is sitting around moping and waiting for the anticipated murder of Fafner. The sound of horse hooves alerts us that someone is coming.

Riding Motif

Alberich hopes it is the dragon killer. He is disappointed when the Wanderer enters the stage; he knows that Wanderer is Wotan. When the Wanderer sees who is present, he greets him as Schwarz Alberich or "Black Alberich." Remember in Act 1, Wotan referred to himself as Light Alberich. He has acknowledged, then, that both he and Alberich are doomed by the curse of the Ring. Of course, we knew this early on from the similarities of the Ring Motif, the Ring having been made by Alberich; and the Valhalla Motif, Valhalla having been created by Wotan's will.

Ring Motif

Valhalla Motif

Wotan has finally accepted his fate. He remarks that he has discarded his schemes to save the world; he has only come to watch.

Alberich, on the other hand, wants to get the Ring back in order to regain power and exact revenge on those who have stood in his way. He mulls over his schemes for retrieving the Ring, storming Valhalla, and becoming ruler of the world. Wotan tells Alberich that Mime is the only other person who is interested in the Ring now and that Mime is currently en route, having manipulated Siegfried to follow him to the cave, where he hopes Siegfried will kill the dragon.

Wotan suggests that Alberich negotiate with Fafner: maybe, if Fafner gives the Ring to Alberich, Mime and Siegfried will try killing Alberich instead of bothering Fafner. To Alberich's horror, Wotan wakes Fafner. The two Alberiches, dark and light, warn Fafner that someone is on his way to kill him. If he gives the Ring away, perhaps he could still keep his treasure and, more importantly, his life. Fafner is unfazed and tells them to let him go back to sleep. Wotan laughs and rides away. Alberich slinks aside to watch what will happen.

Scene Two

Mime and Siegfried approach. Mime says Siegfried is sure to learn fear at this place and mentions the terrifying qualities of the dragon, including his poisonous spittle. Siegfried, unimpressed, says if the dragon has a heart, that's where he will strike. Mime explains that the dragon leaves its cave each midday for a drink at the stream. Then he retreats to where he can watch but not be too close to the danger.

Somewhat uncharacteristically, Siegfried quietly lies down under a tree and contemplates things. A bird begins to sing a pretty song.

Wood Bird's Song

Siegfried wants to converse with the bird, so he makes a whistle from a reed. The reed makes a terrible sound, demonstrated by the orchestra's English horn. He throws the reed down in disgust.

Then he has the idea to communicate with the Wood Bird using his hunting horn.

He enjoys playing the music so much that he gets carried away. The horn gets louder and louder and finally wakes up the dragon, who slithers out of the cave. Siegfried confronts him. They argue, then fight, and Fafner ends up with Nothung plunged in his heart. As he is dying, Fafner relates a little of his life and how, with his own demise, the giants' lineage is at an end. He warns Siegfried that the same one who has enticed him to commit this murder (Mime) is now plotting Siegfried's own death. "Take heed!" he says. At the last moment, Siegfried thinks maybe he can learn about his parents from the dragon. But it is too late. Fafner rolls over and dies with Siegfried's name on his lips. (Do dragons have lips?)

When Siegfried draws his sword from Fafner's body, some of the dragon's blood drips onto his hand. It burns like fire! Instinctively, Siegfried brings his hand to his mouth to suck the blood off his fingers. Let's see what happens when *we* taste dragon's blood.

Dragon's Blood

5.5-ounce can of spicy vegetable juice

1 tsp. Worcestershire sauce

Dash onion powder

2 dashes garlic powder

½ tsp. lime-infused salt. Lime-infused salt can be found at some specialty food retailers. You can also make your own by mixing ¼ cup coarse salt with 1 tsp. dried lime (see directions for drying the lemon slices in the Foot Soak recipe).

- Mix all ingredients together.
- Serve.

The Wood Bird is singing again and suddenly Siegfried can understand its song. Tasting the dragon's blood has given him a new power of understanding. The bird advises Siegfried to enter the cave to claim to the treasure he has won, particularly the Tarnhelm and the Ring. "Great!" he says, "Thanks!" And he disappears into the cave.

Scene Three

Alberich and Mime emerge from their hiding places, where they have been watching Siegfried. They bicker about which one of the dwarves will get possession of the Ring. When Siegfried exits the cave carrying the Tarnhelm and the Ring, the dwarves go back to their hiding places. While Siegfried is examining the "trinkets" he has collected, the bird sings again. She tells Siegfried to be wary of Mime. Now that Siegfried has acquired new listening skills, he will be able to understand the meaning behind the words Mime speaks.

Mime comes back onstage. What follows is Wagner's clever depiction of Mime's hypocrisy. Mime's words are dripping with malice, but he sings them to variations of the Brooding motif and his Sob Story Motif, the syrupy, coaxing melody used during Act One. Mime tries to cajole Siegfried into taking a sip of the potion. He says that it will be refreshing after the exhausting battle with the dragon. Mime's tactics are useless, as Siegfried now can hear the meaning behind Mime's words: the potion will put Siegfried to sleep and Mime will use Nothung to kill him. Mime drones on until Siegfried gets fed up with the lies and whining. He strikes Mime with the sword, killing him and fulfilling Wanderer's bequest. We hear Alberich laughing from his hiding place. Brotherly love.

The trombones play the Curse Motif, underscoring another murder that lust for the Ring has incited. Siegfried moves Mime's body into the cave while sarcastically bidding the dead dwarf to enjoy the treasure. Then Siegfried shoves the corpse of the dragon in position to block the cave's entrance.

Our hero is pretty tired now, so he lies down under the tree, ruminating over his lot in life. Doubtless, he is a bit disappointed that he still has not learned what fear is. He realizes that he is lonely and asks the Wood Bird for advice. (I think he is horny, too.)

The Wood Bird knows of the perfect wife for Siegfried. She lies asleep on a rock surrounded by fire. Only someone who is without fear can pass through the fire to awaken the Brünnhilde. (The agitated tone of the music here is convincing: yes, Siegfried is definitely horny.) "Oh joy," says Siegfried, "maybe I can learn fear from Brünnhilde!" Jubilant music ends Act Two as Siegfried follows the Wood Bird offstage.

The Wood Bird deserves a tasty birdseed treat for all the help she has given Siegfried.

Wood Bird Trail Mix

1 tbs. poppy seeds
½ cup diced dried apple
½ cup puffed millet
½ cup hulled sunflower seeds
3 tbs. Mini M&M candies

- Place the apple slices in a bowl.
- Add the poppy seeds and toss or press with the back of a spoon so that most of the seeds stick to the apples.
- Add the millet, sunflower seeds, and candies.
- Mix well.
- Store in an air-tight container and take on your next hike to share with the birds in the woods.

Act Three

Prologue and Scene One

The music that introduces Act Three is powerful. In fact, if I had to choose, the prelude to Act Three would be my favorite two minutes of the whole Ring Cycle. We hear horse hooves, the Riding Motif. Here comes Wotan—we can hear his Spear Motif, as well as Wanderer's slowed-down chord progression. We know he is looking for Erda because her motif winds through the piece. In fact there are about eight motifs in this expertly crafted prelude. Turn the volume up and you'll hear the beautifully rich instrumentation. It is stupendously terrific.

Erda has been sleeping, the only thing she truly likes to do. Wotan has to make a lot of noise near the entrance to her cave to wake her up and, once she's awake, you can be sure that he had better have a darned good reason. I have given a lot of thought to this and, if I were Erda, I can think of precisely one thing that Wotan could say to get me to wake up and come out of my cave to see him:

"Wake up Erda, I have fresh garden tomatoes!"

Heirloom Tomatoes, Polenta, and Mozzarella

1 lb. fresh home-grown tomatoes

8 oz. fresh mozzarella cheese

4 cups water, divided into two portions of 3 cups and 1 cup

1 cup cornmeal

1 tsp. salt

6 tbs. olive oil

1 leek

½ cup fresh basil leaves

½ tsp. dried oregano (or 1 tsp. fresh oregano)

- Place 3 cups of the water in a heavy saucepan, bring to a boil.
- Place the other cup of water (cold water) in a bowl.
- Whisk the cornmeal into the cold water.
- Stirring constantly, add the cornmeal mixture to the boiling water.
- Add the salt. After the mixture comes to a boil, lower the heat.
- Continue cooking and stirring until fairly thick. It takes about 15 minutes.
- Stir in 2 tbs. of the olive oil and then continue to cook and stir until the mixture is stiff, about 15-20 minutes more.
- Spread onto a jelly roll pan so that the polenta is about 3/8" deep. Cool.
- While it is cooling, prepare the garnish:
- Chop the leek and basil. If using fresh oregano, chop it, too.
- Heat 4 tbs. olive oil in a skillet.
- Add the leek, basil, and oregano.
- Cook until the leek is somewhat translucent and the herbs are limp.
- When the polenta is cooled, cut it into rounds or squares.
- Cut the tomatoes into thick slices.
- Slice the cheese.
- Preheat the oven to 400°.
- Use the other 2 tbs. oil to cover the bottom of a shallow baking dish or jelly roll pan.

- Place the polenta pieces in the oiled baking dish.
- Lay a slice of tomato and a slice of cheese over each piece of polenta .
- Top each piece with a small spoonful of sautéed vegetable garnish.
- Bake for about 10 minutes, until the polenta is golden brown and the cheese is melted.
- Serve hot for a light meal or cooled as hors d'oeuvres.

Heirloom Tomatoes, Polenta, and Mozzarella hors d'oeuvres served with citrus-stuffed olives

While Erda is enjoying her lunch, Wotan explains his reasons for interrupting her sleep. He is tired of the Wanderer role and of just observing without acting. He wants to try once more to see if he can fix things to prevent what Erda has predicted: that "all that is will end." He tells her she is the only one who has the knowledge he needs.

Not all the way awake, she is grumpy. So she answers, "Go ask the Norns." The Norns are Erda's ancient daughters who weave people's destiny, similar to the Fates in ancient Greek mythology. Erda dreams, the dreams are transmitted to the Norns as threads, and the Norns braid the threads into the Rope of Fate. Since the Norns only *manifest* Erda's thoughts and dreams, this answer is not good enough for Wotan because, by the time the Norns' cord has been woven, destiny will already be fixed. Wotan needs some information immediately because he must act now, before it is too late. "How do I hold back a rolling wheel?" he asks.

Still grumpy, Erda says, "Well, you could ask Brünnhilde. She is fearless and pretty insightful." Then, of course, Wotan has to explain why he can't ask Brünnhilde.

"What???" Erda responds. She is disgusted and declares, "This world is too much for me."

Erda's frustration with Wotan is understandable. She did try to help him. Twice he jeopardized the world order 'way back in *The Rhinegold*: first, when he defied love by offering Freia as payment to the Giants, and then when he paid the Giants with the Ring instead of giving it back to the Rhine Maidens. When Erda advises him, he only accepts part of her counsel and then he wants her to fix the consequences. Now he claims to have given up dominion over the world—to be the "Wanderer" who is just watching—but he still refuses to relinquish power. (I assume that she is quite miffed at Wotan's treatment of Brünnhilde, too.) She has shared her wisdom with him in the past, but says she can't do anything for him now. He should just leave her alone and let her go back to sleep.

"No way, not yet," says Wotan. He accuses Erda of having reawakened his heart—for having planted concern for the world in him—when she convinced him that keeping the Ring would have destructive consequences. He wants to know how to reverse things, to conquer his concern for the world so he doesn't care anymore.

At this point, the discussion degenerates into bickering. Erda says he is a hypocrite; he is the epitome of defiance, yet he punishes defiance in others. He calls her a hypocrite, too, and says that if she thinks she's so smart, she should remember that he still has enough power to send her back into the earth to sleep undisturbed forever, so there! (I am paraphrasing.)

Anyway the gist of this scene, which started out so magnificently and has ended up sounding like a sandbox quarrel, is that Wotan comes to terms with some facts and makes a decision. He will bequeath the world to Siegfried because Siegfried, who now has the Ring, is invulnerable to its curse. As long as Siegfried stays innocent, in love, and free from greed, he cannot be influenced by the Ring. Wotan makes his own prediction by doing what he always did best: stating his will. Siegfried will find Brünnhilde, wake her up, and she will do what has to be done in order to redeem the world. Erda goes back into the earth and, evidently, she does sleep forever because we don't see her again.

Sketch for costume designs for the 1878 Bayreuth production of *Der Ring des Nibelungen* by Carl Emil Doepler (1824-1905).
Public domain.

Scene Two

Wotan, as Wanderer, hangs around the rocky cliff near the place where he left Brünnhilde. He is waiting for Siegfried, who approaches led by the Wood Bird. The Wood Bird is frightened of Wanderer and flutters away. Wanderer asks Siegfried where he's going. Thinking that the stranger might be able to tell him which way to go now that the Wood Bird has left, Siegfried approaches Wanderer and asks if he knows the way to a rock surrounded by fire where a woman sleeps. Wanderer wants to know how he found out about this woman.

"A little bird told me," says Siegfried.

Wanderer wants to know how he could understand the bird's song and Siegfried relates his adventure with the dragon. Wanderer asks several questions. Siegfried tells him about Mime, the sword, and its fragments. He also asks Wanderer some rather impertinent questions.

Wanderer chides Siegfried by telling him that respect is due to an old man, but nonetheless he indulges Siegfried's questions. He explains the reason that he wears his hat and he explains that Siegfried is looking at him with the same eye that he has lost. (This riddle-like comment is full of symbolism about Siegfried being a secondary embodiment of Wotan's will.) Siegfried chuckles and says at least Wanderer is good for a laugh, but now he should give him directions to his destination or get out of his way. During their exchange, a fiery glow grows in intensity behind them.

Wanderer, still having misgivings about giving up absolute power, forbids Siegfried to proceed and Siegfried threatens the old man with Nothung. Wanderer tries to frighten Siegfried with scary talk about the fire, but Siegfried is not afraid of fire. Wanderer says that his spear, the same one that shattered Nothung, will prevent him from going any farther.

"If this is the spear that shattered Nothung, then you are my father's enemy! What a great opportunity for vengeance!" cries Siegfried. He strikes Wanderer's spear and it breaks.

"I can no longer stop you," says Wotan. Having his spear smashed will have more of an emotional impact on Wotan than he expected, putting him in a profoundly gloomy mood. But for now, he gathers up the pieces of his spear and disappears. The fire around Brünnhilde is very bright now.

Carl Perron (1858-1928) as Wotan in Die Walküre (1896, photographer unkown). Public domain.

Siegfried wonders—for all of about 2 seconds—where the stranger has gone but he is distracted by the fire and continues on toward Brünnhilde, plunging into the flames while playing his horn. During the transition from Scene Two to Scene Three, the orchestra plays the Magic Fire Motif, highlighted by the Wood Bird's Song, Siegfried's Motif, Siegfried's Horn Call, and finally the Magic Sleep Motif. This passage is another wonderful example of Wagner's compositional mastery.

Scene Three

Siegfried emerges from the fire into the same scene we saw at the end of *The Valkyrie*. He sees a horse and then the bright reflection from brilliant, shining metal attracts his attention to a warrior dressed in armor and lying very still. Siegfried has never seen a woman before, much less one with weapons and dressed in helmet and armor, and he assumes this is a man.

The woodwinds are playing slow and soft. Siegfried sings, "I am sure this stuff is heavy. He'll be more comfortable if I remove it." When he removes the helmet, flowing curls are released. When he cuts the coat of mail away from the sleeping form, Brünnhilde's lovely figure in a flowing dress is revealed. Yikes! Suddenly the strings play loud furious music. Frightened, our up-to-now intrepid Siegfried shrieks, *"Das ist kein Mann!"* ("That is no man!").

Das ist kein Mann!

Wagnerites everywhere may call me a heretic, but I think Wagner made a mistake—yes, he goofed—with that part of the libretto. This is a profoundly dramatic scene but Siegfried's line breaks the dramatic tension. The audience knows that this is Brünnhilde and Siegfried should have guessed it because nobody else is inside the circle of fire, and how many circles of magic fire could there be? His statement, his reaction, and the tune are silly and the audience always laughs. The humor distracts us from identifying with the hero's profound transformation. Surely there is another way to demonstrate Siegfried's first experience of fear in a way that sustains the intensity of the moment. But this is what Wagner wrote, so this is what we have.

Astonished, Siegfried cries for help and sings about his terror. (Give me a break, Siegfried. It's not like she attacked you.) He gets past his fear eventually and tries waking the sleeping Brünnhilde. Finally he kisses her and she opens her eyes.

Siegfried und Brünnhilde, 1909, by Charles Ernest Butler (1864-1933). Public domain.

Brünnhilde's awakening music is ethereally beautiful. The Fate, or Death, Motif is transformed into awakening life-affirming music that seems to reach to the heavenly heights.

Awakening

Beautifully, she greets the day and then asks who has awakened her. Siegfried and Brünnhilde meet. They proclaim their love and devotion for about twenty minutes.

Wagner's Siegfried at the Italian Royal Opera, Covent Garden, "The Awakening of Brunnhilde."
(Cover of *The Illustrated London News* June 18, 1892.) Public domain.

We need something to eat while they are gabbing, so let's fix something that is sweet and encircled by fire like Brünnhilde: Flaming Mangoes with Cardamom Syrup. Since it is probably hot inside that circle of fire, it will be nice to have some ice cream with it. If you feel like making your own, the Custardy Vanilla Ice Cream accompanies the Flaming Mangoes deliciously.

Flaming Mangoes with Cardamom Syrup

8 cardamom pods, hulled

½ tsp. lemon zest

1 cup water

½ cup light brown sugar, firmly packed

2 ripe mangoes

¼ cup rum

- Crush the cardamom seeds with a mortar and pestle.
- Place the cardamom and lemon zest in a large frying pan.
- Add water and sugar.
- Cook over high heat, stirring constantly, until the sugar dissolves.
- Lower heat and boil gently until sugar syrup is reduced about half, about 10 minutes.
- You should have about ½ cup cardamom syrup.
- Peel and cut mangoes lengthwise into ½-inch slices.
- Add the mango slices to the hot syrup.
- Cook over high heat for about 3 minutes. Turn the slices so that they are evenly heated.
- In a separate, smaller pan, warm the rum until it is hot.
- Ignite the rum and pour over mangoes.
- Serve by spooning the mangoes and flaming syrup over the vanilla ice cream.

Custardy Vanilla Ice Cream

4 egg yolks

1 pint heavy cream

½ cup caster sugar or granulated sugar

1 vanilla bean

- If you can't find caster sugar, it's easy to make your own. Place the granulated sugar in a food processor or blender and pulse for 10 seconds or so. *Voilà*, caster sugar: finer than granulated but coarser than powdered.
- Pour half the cream (1 cup) into a saucepan. Set aside the other cup of cream.
- Bring the cream just to the boiling point over low heat but do not boil.
- Turn off the heat and cover the pan.
- Flatten the vanilla bean on a cutting board and open it by making a slice in it lengthwise. Do not remove the insides of the bean.
- Add the vanilla bean to the cream, set aside to steep.
- Mix the egg yolks and sugar in a mixing bowl and beat until thick.
- After the cream and vanilla have cooled for 30 minutes, remove the vanilla bean pod from the cream. If any seeds remain in the pod, scrape them out and add them back to the cream. Discard the pod.
- Whisking the egg mixture constantly, slowly pour in the cooled cream from the pan.
- Pour the custard mixture back into the pan and warm over low heat. Do not boil.
- Stir constantly until the mixture thickens.
- When the mixture is thick enough to coat the back of a spoon, turn off the heat and move the pan to another surface where it can cool. When the pan is cool enough, it can be refrigerated.
- When completely cooled, or even cold, stir in the rest of the cream.
- Pour the entire mixture into your ice cream maker and freeze, following the manufacturer's instructions.

Good grief, they are still singing. You may have already noticed that, prior to this scene, the only times we have heard two or more voices singing together, the singers were either the Rhine Maidens or the Valkyries. Each team of ladies is interrelated enough to be thought of as a composite character. Now, however, when Brünnhilde and Siegfried sing together, it symbolizes their unity of spirit[2] and, well, you can tell from the frantic music that they are *both* horny now. Let's leave them alone.

_____

[2] Greenberg, lecture 12.

TWILIGHT OF THE GODS

Prologue

At the beginning of the Prologue, the orchestra plays the awakening music we heard after Siegfried first kissed Brünnhilde. This beautiful opening is followed by the Fate Motif and then the Weaving Motif, which introduces us to the Norns. They have been mentioned before, but this is the first time we see them. They are weaving the Rope of Fate.

Weaving Motif

While they are weaving, the Norns will need something to eat. Let's bake a bread with a weaving theme: braided Limpa.

Nornish "Not-Quite" Limpa

Limpa is Swedish rye bread. This is not authentic rye bread, but it has similar seasonings and the recipe has the distinct advantage of being fairly easy.

1 3-pound package of frozen bread dough (Frozen dough is readily available in white or whole wheat; if you can find *rye* at your grocer, try that for a more authentic limpa.)

1 tbs. caraway seed

1½ tsp. fennel seed

1½ tsp. anise seed

Grated peel of 1 orange

1 egg

2 tbs. molasses

- Thaw the bread dough according to the package directions.
- Grate the orange peel.
- Mix together the spices and orange peel, set aside.
- When dough is soft enough to knead, separate into 3 equal pieces. If the dough came in three 1-pound loaves, use the loaves as your three pieces.
- Make shallow cuts in the dough. Using ⅓ of the spice mixture for each piece, sprinkle into cuts and gently knead together.

- Shape the dough sections into long ropes of equal length.
- Braid the ropes together.
- Leave the shape in a long braid or, for added effect, form the braid into a ring shape.
- Let rise for 20-30 minutes.
- Preheat oven to 350°.
- Mix egg and molasses in a small bowl.
- Lightly brush the dough with the egg mixture.
- Bake for 15 minutes at 350°.

- Brush the bread with the remainder of the egg mixture.
- Lower oven to 325° and bake for another 20-30 minutes until golden brown.

The glow of Brünnhilde's fire colors the stage because the Norns are weaving their rope on the Valkyrie's Rock. The Norns lament that they had to relocate to this new place. They used to weave under the World Ash Tree, using its strength to fasten and support the Rope of Fate but the sacred Tree is no more and the nearby spring has dried up.

The Norns then give us a Wagnerian (i.e. long) summary of the events to date, beginning before the events in *The Rhinegold*. Long ago, Wotan, having sacrificed an eye for the privilege, came to drink from the spring. The spring's water bestowed wisdom on those willing to pay the high price of an eye for a sip. The knowledge Wotan gained was essential to his role as chief of the gods. While he was at the spring, he broke a branch from the World Ash Tree to use as his spear. Wotan carved records of all the divine proceedings and treaties on the spear. Now the spear has been shattered and the records are in splinters.

The breaking of the branch caused a wound in the tree that never healed. Eventually the tree withered and died. After the spear was broken by Siegfried, Wotan ordered the World Ash Tree cut into pieces. Now the tree is gone and the spring completely dried up. Wotan has called all the gods and heroes to Valhalla, and the logs from the World Ash Tree are stacked up around the fortress. The Norns mourn their loss and, as they sing, they foretell the future: they see the fiery demigod Loge, the destruction of Valhalla, and the collapse of the gods' rule.

Gradually they begin to have trouble seeing clearly and eventually can no longer distinguish the strands that they are weaving. They cannot read its predictions; the rope becomes tangled; and—oh no!—it snaps. When the Rope of Fate breaks, the orchestra reminds us of the reason with the Curse Motif:

Curse Motif

The Norns' work is at an end. They wind the shreds of the Rope of Fate around themselves and disappear underground to join their mother, Erda.

The Norns Disappear, 1911, by Arthur Rackham (1867-1939). Public domain.

Now it is dawn and we join Brünnhilde and Siegfried who are now a fairly normal, if isolated and heroic, passionate married couple. Well, maybe not normal.

We are introduced to Brünnhilde's Motif. Wagner grants her this new theme now that she is mortal and is no longer authorized to use the Valkyrie Motif.

Brünnhilde's Motif

Brünnhilde's fire has been raging for more than two decades, keeping the forest warm and creating a whole new microclimate. Surely that's plenty of time, in this alternate universe, for coconut palms and bananas to have grown. It's time for breakfast.

Tropical Pancakes with Coconut Syrup

2 tbs. sugar

½ cup water

½ cup coconut cream (sometimes called creamed coconut)

2 tbs. butter

1 cup vanilla yogurt

1 egg

1 cup flour

½ cup sugar

2 tsp. baking powder

¼ tsp. salt

1 ripe banana (a firm banana does not yield a good flavor)

- Prepare the coconut syrup:
  - o Mix the water and 2 tbs. sugar together in a small saucepan.
  - o Heat until the sugar dissolves.

- o Cool slightly.
  - o Stir in the coconut cream. (Coconut milk is not thick enough to yield a nice syrupy texture.)
  - o Pour into a small pitcher and set aside.
- Melt the butter and let it cool a bit.
- Mix together the melted butter, yogurt, and egg in a mixing bowl.
- In a separate mixing bowl, combine the flour, baking powder, sugar and salt.
- Add the dry ingredients to the bowl with the egg and yogurt mixture. The batter will be thick.
- Slice the banana and fold most of it into the batter. You can save some for garnish if you like.
- Pour the batter onto a hot griddle or frying pan and cook until the edges are dry.
- Flip and cook the other side until nicely browned.
- Serve the pancakes with the coconut syrup and sliced tropical fruit.

Now that Brünnhilde and Siegfried have had breakfast, they are ready for the day. Siegfried, the hero, has been taking it easy on this rock long enough. He craves adventure. Brünnhilde has taught him all she knows and has given him everything she has to give, even her horse. It is time for him to go out into the world and do whatever it is that professional heroes do.

Before he leaves, Siegfried pledges that he will always be mindful of Brünnhilde and that all his deeds will be in her honor. He gives her the Ring as a sacred token of his eternal love. Brünnhilde bids him good-bye, knowing he will be safe because he is protected from harm in battle by her magic. (Beats me how she has access to magic now that she has lost her divinity.) Siegfried knows Brünnhilde will be safe from intruders because he is the only one fearless enough to go through the fire that surrounds her. With much noise, they part. Siegfried and Grane go forth to adventure.

Siegfried's raft may not have had sails but, what the heck, we can embellish.
Andenken an den Rhein (Rhine River Souvenir), 1840, by J. J. Tanner (1807-1862). Public domain.

Act One

In the great hall of the Gibichungs . . . hmm, let's pause the story for a minute. The Gibichungs seem to have appeared out of nowhere.

Up to now, the *Ring Cycle* has been populated with gods, demi-gods, heroes, magical swords and spears, and sundry divine characters. *Twilight of the Gods* takes place in our world and most of the characters, even Brünnhilde, are human.

The people of the Gibichung clan occupy a territory along the Rhine River. The Gibichung nobility, descended from King Gibich, includes King Gunther and his sister Gutrune. Their trusted advisor is their elder half-brother Hagen. Before she married King Gibich, Lady Grimhilde, their mother, accepted a bribe from Alberich the dwarf. The bribe must have involved a hefty sum for her to agree to have his child. (Yes, Alberich foreswore love; evidently he did not foreswear procreation.) Wagner does not give us any details, but the bribe seems to have been enough for Grimhilde to attain the accoutrements—fortune, clothes, magic potions, and whatever—to nab King Gibich. In any event, the result of the bribing activity was Hagen. Hagen, then, is the son of Alberich prophesied by Erda in Act Two of *The Valkyrie*. Hagen is shrewd and manipulative. He has one objective in life: gaining possession of the Ring. Now we can resume the story.

Scene One

In the great hall of the Gibichungs, Gunther is sitting around wondering how he can increase his fame. He asks Hagen for advice because, although Gunther inherited the throne, Hagen is the brains of the family. Hagen advises his half-siblings to get married. Overly concerned with appearances, they don't know where to find suitable prospects. But Hagen knows of a noble woman, Brünnhilde, who lives in a clearing surrounded by fire. Only the man who braves the fire can be her suitor.

Unadventurous Gunther knows he is not up to the task, but Hagen tells him that there is a fearless hero named Siegfried who would be able to do it. Gunther and Gutrune learn about Siegfried—his parentage, his dragon slaying, his seizure of the Nibelung treasure—everything about him *except* the fact that Siegfried has already found and wed Brünnhilde.

Hagen then suggests that Siegfried would make a perfect husband for Gutrune. Gutrune is hurt by her half-brother's suggestion, assuming it was ironic. She is aware that she has neither the charming personality nor the good looks to attract such a hero and entice him to marry her. But scheming Hagen is full of ideas today. If Gutrune gives Siegfried their mother's magic love-and-forgetting potion, he will be hers.

Magic Potion Motif

Gunther praises his half-brother's ingenuity. Just then, what do we hear echoing from the river but Siegfried's horn!

Siegfried's Horn Call

Scene Two

Siegfried is invited in as an honored guest. Hagen signals to Gutrune to fetch the potion; she does not witness the first conversation between Siegfried, Gunther, and Hagen.

Inside the hall, Gunther offers Siegfried eternal friendship. In a flowery medieval speech Gunther tells Siegfried, "*Mi casa es su casa,*" and promises to be Siegfried's faithful sidekick. Although Siegfried says he has nothing like Gunther's lands and vassals to offer in return, he will swear an oath of friendship on his trusty sword.

Hagen slyly mentions a rumor that they have heard about the Nibelung treasure. Siegfried says that it held so little value to him that he almost forgot about it. He just took a couple of trinkets away and left the rest in a cave guarded by a frightful dead dragon. Hagen recognizes one trinket, the Tarnhelm tucked into Siegfried's belt, and explains its power to shape-shift and teleport the wearer. (This is the first we know of its Star Trek-like transporter beaming capability. If Alberich had known about that, the story would have ended with the second act of *The Rhinegold.*) But what Hagen really wants to know is where the Ring is. Siegfried says it is safe with a glorious woman. Hagen knows that woman is Brünnhilde, but Gunther does not.

Gutrune enters carrying a drinking horn filled with the forgetting potion. Before Siegfried drinks, he swears an oath of love and loyalty to Brünnhilde. He says, "If I were to forget everything you gave me, one lesson I shall never lose. This first drink is to true remembrance: Brünnhilde, I drink to you." He says this to himself; it is important to note that only the whole audience can hear him, not the other characters onstage.

Siegfried hands the drinking-horn back to Gutrune and gazes at her with sudden passion, 1911, by Arthur Rackham (1867-1939). Public domain.

He takes a sip of his drink and suddenly all he can see is Gutrune. The orchestra accompanies this event with the agitated music that signaled "horny!" earlier. What kind of potion could have enough power to make Siegfried forget Brünnhilde, to whom he has sworn eternal devotion and to whom he has given the Ring? Absinthe!

"After the first glass of absinthe you see things as you wish they were. After the second you see them as they are not. Finally you see things as they really are, and that is the most horrible thing in the world." Oscar Wilde[3]

---

[3]Leverson, page 39.

Absinthe

To prepare absinthe properly, gather your supplies. You will need:

Bottle of absinthe

Carafe of ice water

Cool-looking glass, preferably sitting on a snazzy saucer

Slotted spoon (if you are really into being authentic, an absinthe spoon)

Sugar cubes

- Pour one ounce of absinthe into the glass.
- Place the spoon over the glass.
- Put a couple sugar cubes on the spoon.
- Wet the sugar with several drops of water and wait a few moments until the sugar starts to dissolve.
- Slowly drizzle the cold water over the sugar so that the sweetened water dribbles into the glass.
- As the water combines with the absinthe, a *louche*, or cloud, is created in the glass. Part of the absinthe ritual is to take your time enjoying the changes in the color of the louche.
- When four ounces of water have been added, allow the mixture to rest for a minute or two.
- Stir in the rest of the sugar with the spoon.

Siegfried chugged his potion, but it is recommended
that absinthe be sipped slowly in order to enjoy the full flavor experience.

Under the influence of the absinthe love potion, Siegfried sees Gutrune and his marital status as he wishes they were: no ties to prevent him from snuggling with Gutrune, the most ravishing beauty he has ever seen. (Incidentally, as far as the we know, Gutrune is only the second *woman* Siegfried has ever seen, the other being an armored warrior maiden whom he at first mistook for a man.) He declares his love and passion. Then, as an afterthought, he asks Gunther what his sister's name is. "Gutrune," says Gunther simply. Without pausing, Siegfried asks her to marry him. She is embarrassed. Prompted by a meaningful glance from Hagen, she leaves the room in confusion.

Siegfried offers to do something for Gunther in return for his sister's hand in marriage. It just so happens that Gunther would like to get married as well, but the woman he has in mind is surrounded by fire. Siegfried, oblivious that he has ever heard the name "Brünnhilde," promises to help Gunther and they come up with the Tarnhelm Plot. Gunther and Siegfried will travel up the Rhine to Brünnhilde's rock. Using the Tarnhelm, Siegfried will take on the appearance of Gunther, pass through the fire, grab Brünnhilde, and bring her back to the real Gunther. Brünnhilde will think that Gunther rescued her and she will never know that Siegfried was there at all. Great idea, let's drink to it! Gunther and Siegfried are in earnest about this pact and about their friendship. Each makes a cut in his arm with his sword and lets several drops of blood fall into a drink offered by Hagen. Siegfried toasts, "I drip this refreshing blood, flowering life, into the drink!"

Blood Brotherhood

Blü - hen-den Le-bens la - ben-des Blüt träu-felt' ich in den Trank.

They swear blood brotherhood over what, in the libretto, is a horn of wine. For our purposes, it is Siegfried's second glass of absinthe. With blood.

Herbert Janssen (1892-1965) as Gunther, 1934. (Photographer unknown). Public domain.

Bloody Absinthe

Clear absinthe

Hibiscus tea or dried hibiscus flowers (Red Zinger tea bags work fine)

Carafe of ice water

Absinthe glass and spoon, or appropriate substitutes

Sugar cubes

- Pour some clear absinthe into a separate pitcher, about a pint. It is best to use clear absinthe; the "green fairy" kind does not yield a good color.
- Steep 1 tsp. hibiscus flowers or 2 hibiscus tea bags in the pitcher for 20-30 minutes.
- Prepare the drink as in the earlier absinthe recipe with ice water and sugar.
- The hibiscus cuts the strong licorice flavor a bit and adds a very nice aftertaste.

Since the drink that Gutrune prepared for him, Siegfried has been seeing things as he wishes they were. Now, as Oscar Wilde describes, he sees things as they are not. This makes it possible for him to treat his dearest love, Brünnhilde, with the unfeeling cruelty we will witness soon.

Gunther and Siegfried depart immediately, sailing up the Rhine toward Brünnhilde's rock. (Siegfried is horny again and can't delay a moment.) Hagen stays behind and salivates in anticipation of the Ring.

Scene Three

We are back on the rock with Brünnhilde. She is settling down for lunch.

Tropical Salad with Key Lime Vinaigrette

Key Lime Vinaigrette Dressing:
4 to 5 key limes
2 tbs. water
1 cup olive oil
Salt and pepper to taste

Salad:
1 avocado
1 mango
1 banana
1 kiwi fruit
A few kumquats
3-5 large butter lettuce leaves
Cilantro or arugula for garnish
Flour tortilla, naan, pita, or chapatti

- Make the dressing
  - Squeeze enough limes to make 6 tbs. lime juice
  - Combine the lime juice, water, olive oil, salt and pepper in a jar.
  - Shake or whisk immediately before serving.
- Slice the fruit and toss together.
- Splash very lightly with dressing.
- Arrange in a bowl over the lettuce leaves and add more dressing as desired, or fold into the flat bread for a wrap-style sandwich.

Just as she is ready to eat, Brünnhilde hears Waltraute's horse, signaled by the Riding Motif with hints of the Valkyries' Motif. She is certain that her sister has come to tell her of Wotan's forgiveness. She chatters excitedly to Waltraute about having disobeyed Wotan and about being in love, yakkety yak. When she slows down enough for Waltraute to get a word in, she learns that she was quite mistaken. Waltraute informs Brünnhilde about the latest scoop from Valhalla.

Wotan left Valhalla for a very long time, roaming around as Wanderer. When he came home, humiliated, his spear was in pieces. His rule was at an end and Erda's prediction is now transpiring: all things that are—are ending. He ordered the World Ash Tree to be cut down and its logs to be piled up around Valhalla. Then he assembled all the divine and resurrected residents. The gods and heroes are now gathered in Valhalla's throne room, waiting in apprehension for some momentous announcement, but Wotan just sits there silently brooding. He ignores the gods and goddesses, the Valkyries, the heroes, and the Golden Apples. Evidently, Wotan wants to hurry the process along, but he still has his moments of ambivalence about having given up control. Waltraute overheard Wotan whispering to himself, "If she would give back the Ring to the Rhine Maidens, the world would be freed from its curse." Once she heard that, Waltraute hightailed it to Brünnhilde's rock.

Waltraute Confronts Brünnhilde: "The ring upon thy hand—be implored! For Wotan fling it away!"
1911, by Arthur Rackham (1867-1939). Public domain.

Waltraute pleads with Brünnhilde to give up the Ring. Brünnhilde no longer understands the ways of the gods and has the limited perspective of a mortal woman. Ostensibly, she is thoroughly human and therefore values Siegfried's love above anything else. For her, giving up the Ring is tantamount to giving up love itself. She will never give up the Ring, gift of Siegfried and symbol of his eternal love and devotion. The extreme irony here is that, to the other characters involved—including Siegfried, as we shall see very soon—the Ring is a symbol of power that requires the *denial* of love.

Waltraute leaves in a huff; Brünnhilde advises her not to let the door slam against her haunches.

Brünnhilde's chat with Waltraute has delayed her lunch enough that she is ready for an early dinner. Just as she is getting back to her salad, someone else comes to visit. The visitor is entering through the wall of fire, so Brünnhilde assumes that it is Siegfried. When she sees it is a stranger, she lets out a Wagnerian (i.e. loud) scream. She doesn't know that it is Siegfried wearing the Tarnhelm. He has disguised his appearance and his voice so that he appears to be Gunther, one of those plebian chumps she had hoped to avoid. While Siegfried is disguised as Gunther, he sings in the lower parts of the *heldentenor* range, assuming the voice of a baritone to further deceive Brünnhilde.

Brünnhilde, with good reason, is frightened. Asleep for so many years and then awakened to passionate love, her banishment has not seemed as insufferable as she had initially feared. Now, however, this stranger has shown up. He claims her as his own and forcibly seizes the Ring from her while the orchestra plays the Curse Motif. He says that the Ring gives "Gunther" a husband's privileges. This is terrifying and humiliating. Now she understands the true meaning of Wotan's punishment. (Just wait, Brünnhilde. It gets worse.) She has lost her appetite completely.

It is very late, so they retire to her boudoir-cave for the night. To ensure chastity, Siegfried-as-Gunther places Nothung between them while they sleep. Is it so dark that Brünnhilde is unable to recognize Siegfried's illustrious sword? Why don't they just go back to Gunther on the boat immediately? Will Brünnhilde actually get any sleep after missing her lunch and dinner? Wagner does not answer these questions; we must overlook the illogical elements of the story and go on.

Act Two

Scene One

This scene takes place later the same night back in the Hall of the Gibichungs. Hagen is asleep—sort of asleep anyway—and his father, Alberich, comes for a visit. It is not clear if this a real, in-the-flesh visit or a dream. Several times during this scene, Alberich asks Hagen if he is sleeping but Hagen never directly answers that question. In response he only asks, "What do you have to say to my sleep?"

Schläfst du,   Ha - gen mein   Sohn?

Alberich briefly reviews parts of the story for the audience members who may have forgotten about him by now. We haven't seen him since the second act of *The Valkyrie*. He reminds Hagen of his filial duties and that they will share power over the world when Alberich gets the Ring back. Hagen responds that he's working on it, just a bit more patience will get them the prize for which they have conspired for such a long time. Given that both Alberich and Hagen are self-serving and manipulative, I am skeptical of their mutual trust, but that doubt is not part of the story.

Carl Grengg (1853-1914) as Hagen in an early Bayreuth production of *Götterdämmerung.*
(Photo by W. Höffert studio.) Public domain.

It is interesting to note that Hagen is being used as a pawn in Alberich's schemes to recapture the Ring in much the same manner as Wotan formed Siegmund for his plan to restore balance to the world. This seems to be another example of Wotan and Alberich being parallels rather than opposites. Wagner is not explicit about matters such as this in his stories because he felt that music could better communicate what he wanted to relate. As he said in a letter to a friend, "to make my intention too obvious would get in the way of a genuine understanding."[3]

Scene Two

Morning dawns on the Hall of the Gibichungs to the beautiful music of the Dawn Motif.

Dawn Motif

Siegfried appears from nowhere through the magic of the Tarnhelm. He greets Hagen with a cheerful "Hoi-ho!" and tells him that the others are coming "more slowly by boat." Hagen calls Gutrune to join them and Siegfried tells them about his adventure. Now that he has done this favor for Gunther, Siegfried and Gutrune can be married. But first Gutrune has a few questions about last night, Siegfried-as-Gunther's pre-wedding night. Siegfried assures her there was no hanky-panky because Nothung lay separating Brünnhilde and himself all night. Gutrune is satisfied and asks Hagen to call the people to the royal courtyard for a wedding celebration. Gutrune is looking forward to having a sister-in-law and she prepares to welcome Brünnhilde.

[3] Donnington, p.31.

Maude Fay (1878-1964), as Gutrune in Wagner's *Götterdämmerung*. (About 1915, photographer unknown.)
Public domain.

Scene Three

Hagen gets to show off that powerful bass voice of his and we hear something new. So far, we have mostly heard individual voices performing one at a time, but now the vassals sing as a chorus. In a large production, there might be more than 50 tenors and baritones on the stage singing together. It is terrific.

The way in which Hagen announces the wedding is less terrific. It may be an example of Wagner's sense of humor, if he had one. Hagen calls the vassals to gather their arms and prepare for battle. These lyrics have been translated into English to emphasize how alarming the announcement must be to the vassals.

Hagen Calls the Vassals

Hoi-ho — Hoi-ho - ho - ho Ye Gib - ich vas-sals gath-er ye

here. Arms, men! — Arm your-selves! Wea - pons! Wea - pons!

The vassals jump out of bed or interrupt their breakfast, worried that they are being attacked. But, no, after stringing them along for a while Hagen finally tells them that Gunther is traveling home with his valiant bride and they will be married today. The vassals are to prepare the feast. In substance, Hagen scares them out of their wits then tells them it's a wedding, not a war, and they laugh. They sing, "Things must be changing. Hagen the grim made a funny joke." Hilarious. But the music is grand.

Tenor

Gross Glück und Heil lacht nun dem Rhein, da Ha - gen, der

Baritone

Gross Gluck und Heil lacht nun dem Rhein, da Ha - gen der

T.

Grim - me so lu - stig mag sein!

Bar.

Grim - me so lu - stig mag sein!

Scene Four

Gunther enters the scene, virtually dragging Brünnhilde along. The vassals greet them solemnly and they proceed into the hall to meet the other wedding couple, Gutrune and Siegfried. At the mention of Siegfried's name, Brünnhilde looks up from the floor for the first time. She is visibly shocked. The others wonder if Brünnhilde has suddenly become ill.

"What is Siegfried doing here?" she says. Perceiving that he doesn't recognize her, she then spies the Ring on his hand. She asks Gunther why he gave Siegfried the Ring he stole from her, but Gunther says he did not give Siegfried a ring and asks if she is certain it is the same ring. Siegfried boasts that no one gave him the Ring, it was among the loot he won by killing a powerful dragon. Gradually it dawns on Brünnhilde that she has been royally tricked and she is rather displeased. "May the gods guide this rage to break my heart in two in order to smash the one who deceived me!" She proclaims in front of everyone that that Siegfried, not Gunther, is her husband.

This highly dramatic scene shows the once devoted lovers accusing each other of treachery, deceit, and falsehood. Brünnhilde is talking about their past years together, of course, and Siegfried only remembers last night. They both swear an oath of truth on Hagen's spear, vowing death to Siegfried. Yes, even Siegfried pledges his own life as forfeit if he is lying and has broken his promise to Gunther, his blood brother.

The music for the oath is fantastic: loud and dramatic. First Siegfried sings, "Shining Steel! Holy weapon! Witness my everlasting oath!" When he finishes the oath, Brünnhilde grabs the spear point from him and sings the same thing an octave higher.

Oath

Siegfried is very upset by these developments, but nevertheless he tries to allay *Gunther's* fears out of concern for his blood brother. He says that Brünnhilde is confused by the recent events and she will soon calm down and be totally happy as Gunther's wife. The music brightens as Siegfried takes Gutrune's hand and calls to the crowd to follow them to the wedding ceremony. Siegfried, Gutrune, and the vassals exit the stage.

Mmm, a wedding means wedding cookies.

Gibichung Wedding Cookies

½ pound butter

½ cup powdered sugar

2 cups flour

1 tsp. nutmeg

1 tsp. allspice

1 tsp. cloves

½ tsp. salt

More powdered sugar for coating

- In a large mixing bowl, cream together the butter and sugar.
- In a separate mixing bowl, combine the flour, salt, and spices.
- Add the dry ingredients to the butter mixture by half cups, mixing well after each addition.
- If dough is soft, chill in the refrigerator for 1 hour.
- Preheat oven to 350°.
- Form into balls and place on baking sheet.
- Bake 12-15 minutes until the cookies are just beginning to turn golden.
- When cool enough to handle, roll in the powdered sugar.
- Allow to cool completely and roll once again in the powdered sugar.

Scene Five

Brünnhilde, Gunther, and Hagen remain onstage. Brünnhilde is fired up by a rage that the world has never witnessed. She mourns the loss of her divine wisdom, which would have given her the insight to make sense of this situation. As things are, she wonders how she will break the strong bond of love she has for Siegfried. But mostly she is enraged; you know, a woman scorned and all that.

Hagen offers to avenge her. "Oh, right," she thinks, "In your dreams, Hagen." Hagen could not hope to defeat Siegfried. Siegfried is afraid of nothing and furthermore he is protected by every magical art known to Brünnhilde. (Wagner does not explain how Brünnhilde has retained her ability to defend Siegfried with magic spells when, as made clear in Act One, she has lost her divinity and is now human. It is probably best to ignore the many inconsistencies in *Twilight of the Gods.*) Hagen continues to ask questions until Brünnhilde admits that she did not safeguard Siegfried's back because she knew he would never run away from danger. "That's where I'll strike!" Hagen says.

Gunther is distraught with shame and disgrace and begs for help from Hagen, his brainy elder brother. Hagen "helps" by telling him, "You can be helped neither by smarts nor strength. Only Siegfried's death can help you." Hagen's "Siegfried's death!" passage is echoed eerily by the horrified Gunther.

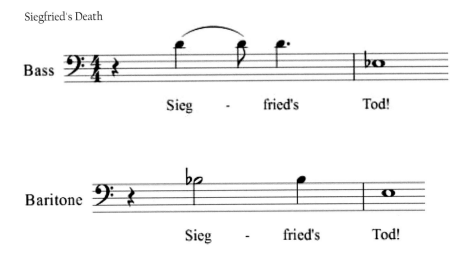

Hagen declares that Siegfried has betrayed them and must pay for his deceit with his life. Brünnhilde, who was deceived by them *all*, says that the death of one will suffice as atonement for every betrayal. As it turns out, this doesn't matter because pretty much everybody bites the dust anyway.

Hagen turns to Gunther, who has misgivings about plotting the murder of his blood brother. Poor Gunther is conflicted. He is not completely convinced that Siegfried is in the wrong. On the other hand, he feels that he should be loyal to Brünnhilde. In addition, he feels terrible about the entire idea because he truly felt loving friendship toward Siegfried and also because he doesn't know how he'll face his sister Gutrune, who loves Siegfried deeply. Hagen prevails upon Gunther to join the plot by tempting him with the Ring. "Immense power will be yours if you get from him the Ring that only death will force him to release," Hagen says, quietly so that Brünnhilde does not hear. The eternal lust for power changes Gunther's mind; he is persuaded.

Hagen suggests a plan. Tomorrow, all the men will go on a hunt. They will murder Siegfried but claim it was the attack of a wild boar that killed him. The oath of revenge that they sing is chilling, musically complicated, and powerful. In the lyrics of their vows, Brünnhilde and Gunther appeal to Wotan for vengeance and justice while Hagen, swearing by Alberich, sings that the Ring and the hoard will soon be his.

Wagner definitely knew how to compose intense endings to his dramatic segments and this is one of his finest. It is best heard loud and live.

Die drei Eidgenossen beim Schwur auf den Rütli (The Three Conspirators), 1790, by Johann Heinrich Füssli (1741-1825). Public domain.

Act Three

There is a short prelude to Act Three, which begins with Siegfried's horn call. After the horn's introduction, the orchestra plays about two minutes of gradually developing arpeggios depicting nature, the Rhine, and the Rhine Maidens. It is the next day and the men have gone hunting in the woods. Siegfried has become separated from the rest of the hunting party and is wandering near the Rhine River.

Scene One

The Rhine Maidens show up near the riverbank and whine about their Rhinegold. The sun's radiance reminds them of the beauty of the gold, which used to shine in the depths of the Rhine just as the sun shines on its surface now. When they hear Siegfried's horn, they call to him and try to convince him to surrender the Ring to them by warning him of its curse. Siegfried thinks he is wise to the manipulative charms of women and takes their warnings as meaningless, even when they predict he will be killed later today. He refuses to give them the Ring. In the grand scheme of things, they conclude, it doesn't matter because they will get their gold back from a proud woman who will inherit the Ring from Siegfried. This comment is too obscure for Siegfried, our thick-headed hero, to understand; he ignores it.

When Siegfried hears Hagen calling, he gathers up his horn and goes off to join the hunters.

Machinery to make it appear that the Rhine Maidens are swimming from *The Ring* premier, Bayreuth, 1876. (Artist unknown). Public domain.

Scene Two

The hunters are taking a rest and preparing a meal with some of the meat from the hunt.

Free-Range Wild Boar Roast

1 boar roast, 3-5 pounds. Wild boar is available from specialty butchers, but a
   pork roast, either shoulder or loin, will work. It's just not what the Gibichungs
   hunted.

Kitchen twine

2 tart apples

½ cup golden raisins

1 fennel bulb

1 onion

2 potatoes

4 carrots

8 Brussels sprouts

1 ripe pear

2-3 cups stock, broth, or bouillon

- Peel, core, and slice the apples.
- Spread the meat out and arrange the apples and raisins lengthwise down
  the middle.
- Roll the meat into a log shape with the apples and raisins inside.
- Tie with kitchen twine at 3" intervals so the roast will keep its shape.
- Place the meat in a roasting pan
- Baste with 1 cup of the stock, set the remainder aside.
- Roast at 375°.
- While the meat is in the oven, slice the fennel bulb, onion, potatoes, Brussels
  sprouts, pear, and carrots.
- After 30-45 minutes, remove the roast from the oven. Lower the heat to
  350°.

- Carefully pour the liquid from the roasting pan into a measuring cup.
- Arrange the sliced vegetables, pear, and any extra apple slices around the meat.
- Baste with the liquid poured from the roasting pan.
- Roast for 1 ¼ to 1 ½ hours at 350°, basting every 20 minutes using the rest of the stock.
- Two hours should yield a nicely cooked roast, but you can use a meat thermometer to check for doneness. Pork is safely cooked when its temperature reaches 145°; be aware that the temperature will continue to rise after the roast is removed from the oven.
- After removing from the oven, allow the meat to "rest" for 5-10 minutes.
- Slice.
- Serve with applesauce, cranberry sauce, or chutney.

Everyone except Gunther has been enjoying the hunt and is savoring the meal. Siegfried offers to entertain the group with stories about his past, hoping the tales will lift Gunther out of the dark mood he is in. He tells stories of his youth in the forest, about forging his own sword, killing the dragon, tasting its blood, understanding the Wood Bird's song, acquiring the Tarnhelm and Ring, and slaying Mime. (Gutrune's magic potion obviously did not affect Siegfried's memories of his life prior to learning about Brünnhilde.)

Before he continues, Hagen offers Siegfried a specially "seasoned" drink to sharpen his memory. Let's recall the quote from Oscar Wilde:

> "After the first glass of absinthe you see things as you wish they were.
> After the second you see them as they are not. Finally you see things
> as they really are, and that is the most horrible thing in the world."

Siegfried's Third Drink of Absinthe

Imagine Hagen preparing this drink at the picnic. Surely he brought crushed ice along in an insulated cooler.

Crushed ice
5 parts absinthe (1 shot)
1 part anisette (1 tbs. or a dash)
Sparkling mineral water or club soda

- Fill a tumbler with crushed ice.
- Add the absinthe and anisette to the ice.
- Finish with sparking water to taste.

The drink is refreshing and restorative—restorative in that it restores Siegfried's memory. Before long he begins to see things "as they really are." When he resumes his story, the music takes on a more lyrical, dreamy quality. He tells the group about the Wood Bird guiding him to Brünnhilde's neck of the woods and how he passed through the fire to find his beautiful wife. He concludes by reminiscing, "Ah, the passion! We embraced like rutting animals in heat."

Even though Gunther knows about the spell Siegfried was under, he is astonished to find out that Siegfried and Brünnhilde have a past together. He is also surprised by what Hagen does next. Did he forget the pact he made the day before, when Hagen pledged to kill Siegfried?

At any rate, this is the moment Hagen has been waiting for. He asks Siegfried, who understands birds' songs, to interpret the calls of two ravens that are soaring above them. When Siegfried stands up to watch the ravens, the Curse Motif roars out from the orchestra and Hagen shouts, "Revenge is what they advise *me*!" as he stabs Siegfried in the back.

Siegfried's Death, 1847, by Julius Schnorr von Carolsfeld, (1794-1872). Public domain.

The men in the hunting party are aghast. A few of them try to hold Hagen back crying, "Hagen, what are you doing?!" Explaining his act as one of avenging a lie, he calmly walks away toward home.

The orchestra plays the Fate Motif followed by—brilliantly—the same music to which Brünnhilde awoke in Act Three of *Siegfried*. Siegfried's dying words are about his beloved Brünnhilde. As night falls, the hunting party packs up and carries Siegfried's corpse back to the Hall of the Gibichungs to the magnificent and tragic music of Siegfried's Funeral.

Siegfried's Funeral

The Death of Siegfried, 1882, by Howard Pyle (1853-1911). Public domain.

Scene Three

We have reached the last part, but don't put your coat on yet, there is still half an hour to go in the opera.

Back at the Hall of the Gibichungs, Gutrune's sleep has been disturbed by frightening dreams. She wanders around looking for something or someone to relieve her anxiety. Siegfried is not home yet and she cannot find Brünnhilde. Just then she hears Hagen calling in the distance. As he approaches, he cruelly tells Gutrune to welcome home her valiant husband. This alarms Gutrune because she didn't hear Siegfried's horn. Nor will she ever hear it again, according to Hagen. Siegfried's body is carried in by Gunther and the hunting party, while Hagen is explaining to Gutrune that the death was caused by a hunting accident—a wild boar attack.

Still from *Die Nibelungen: Kriemhilds Rache*, 1924 film by Fritz Lang (1890-1976). Public domain.

Gunther tries to comfort her, but she turns on him and accuses him of being responsible for Siegfried's death. Quick to transfer the blame, Gunther says, "It wasn't me! Hagen is the 'wild boar' who did the stabbing!" Hagen not only admits it, but he claims that they should thank him for avenging Siegfried's betrayal. And now, he adds, since he has vanquished the "enemy," the spoils are his. He goes for the Ring. Gunther tries to prevent him, insisting that the Ring is Gutrune's inheritance as the widow of Siegfried. Hagen draws his sword and kills Gunther in a brief clash.

When Hagen reaches for the Ring on Siegfried's hand, the dead hero's arm lifts up ominously. This terrifies everybody, even Hagen. (It's lame, but it places a break in the action for Brünnhilde's entrance.)

Solemnly, with great dignity, Brünnhilde comes back onstage. She scolds the group for their petty complaints while the greatest of heroes lies dead in front of them. A short exchange between Gutrune and Brünnhilde clears things up for Gutrune who now understands she was just another dupe in Hagen's malicious plot.

Brünnhilde takes the stage and dominates it for the remainder of the piece. This is another instance of super-hero-caliber performance art; she sings with tremendous passion for about 20 minutes. The music is glorious, the events are extremely dramatic.

Brünnhilde orders a funeral pyre to be built next to the river. She gains insight into all creation and understands everything now—including Wotan's ultimate intentions—and bids her divine father to rest, saying "Rest, rest, you god!"

Rest, Rest

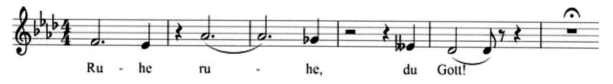

Ru - he ru - he, du Gott!

She removes the Ring from Siegfried's hand; she announces to the Rhine daughters, who are on their way, that the fire will cleanse the gold of its curse before it makes its way back to them; and she then puts the Ring on her own finger. She takes a torch from one of the vassals and throws it onto the pyre. Then she mounts her horse, who has fortuitously shown up. Singing triumphantly, she enters the fire with Grane.

This is a very big fire. It spreads all the way to Valhalla. Everything of the old order burns up. As the Rhine overflows and extinguishes the flames near its banks, the Rhine Maidens come up to retrieve their property. Having escaped the fire, Hagen jumps into the flood shouting to them, "Get away from the Ring!" But he is drowned by two of the Rhine Maidens while the third finds the Ring and holds it up exultantly. The Rhine Maidens have their Rhinegold, Valhalla and its residents go up in flames, and the world is inherited by us humans.

World on Fire, US Department of Agriculture. (2004, photographer unknown.) Public domain.

The orchestral music is gorgeous. It weaves together the motifs of Nature, the Curse, Valhalla, the Spear, the Sword, the Rhine Maidens, Siegfried, and ends sublimely with the Redemption Motif.

Redemption Motif

If you are at a live performance of *Twilight of the Gods*, you have most likely been in the theatre for about six hours now. Surely, you have worked up an appetite. What happens as Valhalla goes up in flames? Time for a barbecue! Grill everything in sight!

Barbecue-Everything-in-sight Salmon Dinner

1 large or several small filets of salmon, 2 pounds total (Enough for 4-6 servings.)

6 shallots

1 pound asparagus spears

1 cucumber, 2 or 3 endives, sliced pineapple

½ cup maple syrup

¼ cup vegetable oil

¼ cup soy sauce

½ cup + 2 tbs. orange juice

2 tbs. butter

- Mix together the maple syrup, oil, soy sauce, and ½ cup orange juice; divide into two portions.

- Marinate the salmon in one portion of the maple syrup mixture.
- Clean and trim the asparagus. Slice the shallots in quarters lengthwise.
- Add the asparagus and shallots to the reserved portion of the marinade.
- Melt the butter and mix with 2 tbs. orange juice.
- Peel and slice the cucumber, wash and cut the endives in half lengthwise.
- Marinate the sliced cucumbers, endive, and pineapple slices in the butter-orange juice mixture.
- Allow the three sets of marinades about an hour in the refrigerator.
- Prepare the grill. When it is hot, carefully lay the fish and the vegetables on the grill. If the spaces in the grill are large, use a grill basket or tray to keep the smaller items from falling into the fire.
- Grill. Check frequently because the vegetables will cook quickly. The salmon takes about 10 minutes on each side.

Enjoy with Brünnhilde's tropical salad and Freia's Golden Apple Risotto for a real après-opéra feast.

The Ring is dramatic and glorious. The ending leaves audience members with an exquisite, almost unearthly feeling of ethereal elevation. This experience is attributable to the music. Familiarity with the story makes the experience of the music more meaningful and profound. However, the story without the music has serious shortcomings.

And that motivates me to encourage you, once again, to listen to this music while reading and learning the story. Please beg, borrow, or buy a recording of *The Ring of the Nibelung* to enrich your understanding. It is just not the same without actually hearing those grand voices accompanied by the giant orchestra performing this magnificent music. Enjoy your ride.

BIBLIOGRAPHY

Here is a list of the publications I used in writing *Nibbling on the Ring* for those who are interested in learning more about *The Ring of the Nibelung*. The most helpful of these are starred.

Armour, Margaret. *The Fall of the Nibelungs*. E. P. Dutton & Co., 1908.

Berger, William. *Wagner Without Fear*. Vintage Books, 1998.

Byock, Jesse L. *The Saga of the Volsungs: The Norse Epic of Sigurd the Dragon Slayer*. University of California Press, 1990.

Camner, James. *The Great Opera Stars in Historic Photographs: 343 Portraits from the 1850s to the 1940s*. Dover Publications, 1978.

Cooke, Derycke. *An Introduction to Der Ring Des Nibelungen.* London Records 1995. Originally released by Decca in 1968. (* Superb guide to the most important leitmotifs.)

Craigie, W. A. *The Icelandic Sagas*. Cambridge University Press, 1913.

Cunningham, Marion. *The Fanny Farmer Cookbook*, 13th edition. Alfred A. Knopf, 1990.

Donington, Robert. *Wagner's Ring and its Symbols*. St Martin's Press 1974.

Evensen, Kristian. *Leitmotifs in Der Ring des Nibelungen: An Introduction.* ‹http://www.trell.org/wagner/motifs.html›. (*This is a good overview of how the motifs transform throughout the work.)

Greenberg, Robert. *The Music of Richard Wagner*. The Teaching Company, 2010. ‹www.thegreatcourses.com›. (*This is an enjoyable summary of Wagner's life and his eleven music dramas.)

Hatto, A. T. *The Niebelungenlied.* Penguin Books, 1969.

Holman, J. K. *Wagner's Ring: A Listener's Companion & Concordance.* Amadeus Press, 1996.

Lee, M. Owen. *Wagner, the Terrible Man and His Truthful Art: The 1998 Larkin-Stuart Lectures.* University of Toronto Press, 1999.

   Wagner's Ring: Turning the Sky Round. Limelight Editions, 1994.

Leverson, Ada. *Letters to the Sphinx from Oscar Wilde: with Reminiscences of the Author.* Duckworth, (3 Henrietta Street, W. C.2) London, 1930. Pages 39-40.

McEwen, Terence. *The Ring of the Nibelung, Summer 2011 Preview.* San Francisco Opera, 2011. (*A set of CDs providing an audio review of the music and story to ticket holders for the Summer 2011 *Ring* performances.)

Queenan, Joe. "Ye gods! An A-Z of Wagner's Ring." *The Guardian,* Thursday 13 September 2007. ‹http://www.theguardian.com/music/2007/sep/14/classicalmusicandopera1›.

Rackham, Arthur. *Rackhams' Color Illustrations for Wagner's "Ring."* Dover Publications, 1979.

Russell, Anna. *The Anna Russell Album.* Columbia Records, 1972.

   The Ring of the Nibelung (An analysis) Parts 1-3. Video from her "The First Farewell Concert, 1984" and audio from her 1953 version. ‹http://www.youtube.com/watch?v=07E5sLsJQe0›.

Ryder, Frank G. *The Song of the Nibelungs: A Verse Translation from the Middle High German Nibelungenlied.* Wayne State University Press, 1962.

Stone, Monte, and Juhan Sonin. *The Ring Disc: An Interactive Guide to Wagner's Ring Cycle,* © 1997 by Media Café Productions. (*Terrific detailed guide to *The Ring,* its motifs, symbols, characters, including the complete score for piano and voices.)

Wagner, Richard. *Actors and Singers.* Translated by William Ashton Ellis. University of Nebraska Press, 1995. Originally published as *Richard Wagner's Prose Works, Volume 5, Actors and Singers,* Kegan Paul, Trench, Trübner & Co., 1896.

   The Dusk of the Gods: Complete Vocal Score and a Facilitated Arrangement. Karl Klindworth, music arranger, English translation by Frederick Jameson. G. Schirmer, 1904, 1899.

   The Rhinegold: Complete Vocal Score in a Facilitated Arrangement. Karl Klindworth, music arranger, English translation by Frederick Jameson. G. Schirmer, 1904, 1899.

   The Ring of the Nibelung. Translated, and with a foreword, by Stewart Robb. Introduction by Edward Downes. Dutton, 1960. (An older translation of the libretto.)

Siegfried: Music-Drama in 3 Acts. Piano reduction by R. Kleinmichel, English translation by H. and F. Corder. Schott & Co., 1899.

The Valkyrie: Complete Vocal Score in a Facilitated Arrangement. Karl Klindworth, music arranger, English translation by Frederick Jameson. G. Schirmer, 1904, 1899.

Wagner's Ring of the Nibelung: A Companion. Spencer, Stewart, and Barry Millington, editors. Thames & Hudson, 1993. (*A newer, modern translation of the libretto.)

ACKNOWLEDGMENTS

Thank you to all who helped in the creation of this book. Thank you, Emily Powell, for your time and expertise in reading and re-reading the text. Your help has been invaluable.

The enthusiastic support and encouragement of the Wagner Society of Santa Fe, especially Yoko Arthur, is greatly appreciated.

Uncredited illustrations are my own photographs. Thank you, Thea Rose Light, for your advice and help with the pictures.

My recipes have been created by trial and error. No recipe has been copied *verbatim* from another source. The only cookbook I included in the bibliography is *The Fanny Farmer Cookbook* because it has been my constant kitchen companion for more than 20 years. However, there are countless now-forgotten sources for the recipes. I am grateful to every friend, cookbook author, and recipe blogger who has offered me ideas. Even though I have forgotten exactly how you helped me, thank you all.

Finally, thank you to Team Guinea Pig: my family, my co-workers, and the students and patrons of Fogelson Library at Santa Fe University of Art and Design for helping to taste-test the recipes.

RECIPE INDEX

Fonts used in this book's design are Californian FB for the text, *Rage Italic for the recipe titles*, and *Segoe Print for the recipe content*. Californian FB was designed by Carol Twombly, David Berlow, and Jane Patterson, published by Font Bureau in 1994, and based on Frederic W. Goudy's California Old Style typeface created for the University of California Press in 1938. Rage Italic was designed by Ron Zwingelberg in 1984 and originally published by ITC/Fontek. Segoe Print was designed by Brian Allen, Carl Crossgrove, James Grieshaber, and Karl Leuthold in 2006 for Ascender/Microsoft Typography.

Software programs used to design the book include Microsoft Word 2013, CreateSpace® templates, Adobe InDesign®, and MuseScore an open source scorewriter developed by Werner Schweer. (Thanks, Werner, Musescore is terrific!)

Made in the USA
San Bernardino, CA
02 February 2016